Comments on other *Amazi*   & reviewers

"Tightly written volumes filled with lots of wit and humour about famous and infamous Canadians."
Eric Shackleton, *The Globe and Mail*

"The heightened sense of drama and intrigue, combined with a good dose of human interest is what sets Amazing Stories *apart."*
Pamela Klaffke, *Calgary Herald*

"This is popular history as it should be... For this price, buy two and give one to a friend."
Terry Cook, a reader from Ottawa, on **Rebel Women**

"Glasner creates the moment of the explosion itself in graphic detail...she builds detail upon gruesome detail to create a convincingly authentic picture."
Peggy McKinnon, *The Sunday Herald*, on **The Halifax Explosion**

"It was wonderful...I found I could not put it down. I was sorry when it was completed."
Dorothy F. from Manitoba on **Marie-Anne Lagimodière**

"Stories are rich in description, and bristle with a clever, stylish realness."
Mark Weber, *Central Alberta Advisor*, on **Ghost Town Stories II**

"A compelling read. Bertin...has selected only the most intriguing tales, which she narrates with a wealth of detail."
Joyce Glasner, *New Brunswick Reader*, on **Strange Events**

"The resulting book is one readers will want to share with all the women in their lives."
Lynn Martel, *Rocky Mountain Outlook*, on **Women Explorers**

CONVOYS OF
WORLD WAR II

AMAZING STORIES®

CONVOYS OF WORLD WAR II

Dangerous Missions on the North Atlantic

HISTORY/MILITARY

by Dorothy Pedersen

With respect and affection, for Bryon Mackie.
You *are* the greatest!

PUBLISHED BY ALTITUDE PUBLISHING CANADA LTD.
1500 Railway Avenue, Canmore, Alberta T1W 1P6
www.altitudepublishing.com
1-800-957-6888

Extreme care has been taken to ensure that all information presented in
this book is accurate and up to date. Neither the author nor the
publisher can be held responsible for any errors.

Publisher	Stephen Hutchings
Associate Publisher	Kara Turner
Editors	Joan Dixon and Heather Hudak
Digital Photo Colouring	Bryan Pezzi

We acknowledge the financial support of the Government
of Canada through the Book Publishing Industry Development
Program (BPIDP) for our publishing activities.

Altitude GreenTree Program
Altitude Publishing will plant twice as many trees as were used
in the manufacturing of this product.

National Library of Canada Cataloguing in Publication Data

Pedersen, Dorothy, 1950-
Convoys of World War II / Dorothy Pedersen.

(Amazing stories)
ISBN 1-55439-002-8

1. Naval convoys--North Atlantic Ocean--History--20th century. 2. Merchant marine--North Atlantic
Ocean--History--20th century. 3. World War, 1939-1945--Naval operations, Canadian. 4. World War,
1939-1945--Campaigns--North Atlantic Ocean. 5. World War, 1939-1945--Personal narratives,
Canadian. I. Title. II. Series: Amazing stories (Calgary, Alta.)

D779.C2P43 2005   640.54'293   C2005-902840-8

Printed and bound in Canada by Friesens
2 4 6 8 9 7 5 3

Contents

Prologue

"Torpedo ahead," the lookout yelled.

With thudding hearts, a pair of Canadian sailors watched the torpedo skim the water in front of their corvette. It was racing straight for the tanker — one of the 35 ships in their convoy and only a hundred metres away. With a deafening impact, the shock of the explosion almost blew the sailors right off their ship.

The tanker's cargo of fuel, destined for the Allies' war efforts in Europe, spewed into the ocean and ignited into a hissing, spitting, roaring fireball. As the tanker burned, the horrified witnesses heard only weak cries. After a short time, these too were drowned out by the thunder of the angry fire. The sailors knew there was no point in the convoy's rescue ship sticking around.

Escorted by armed navy vessels, the convoy of Canadian and British merchant ships raced onward, trying to put distance between them and the visible and invisible dangers of the North Atlantic. Despite the reputed safety of the pack, another of their ships was stricken soon after. This time, there was no fire, but the ship was sinking quickly. Lifeboats had been lowered but some sailors barely had time to grab a life ring before hitting the frigid water. The rescue ship was ordered to stay for them as the rest of the convoy again sailed on.

Choppy seas made the rescue agonizingly slow and difficult. Scramble nets were thrown over the side of the rescue ship for the desperate men to haul themselves aboard. Half an hour later, only a few men and boys had been saved. Many more were losing the fight with the frigid water.

Then the order came that was even more chilling: "Abandon the rescue." Once again under attack, the convoy had signalled for help. The rescue ship revved up its engines.

In the ocean, the weakening hearts of the remaining sailors sank alongside their ship.

Chapter 1
Saving Lives and Easter Eggs

Doug McCarthy
[Royal Canadian Navy V27415]

Packages from caring civilians were a lifeline to Canadian sailors during World War II. Socks or scarves, candies and chocolate — accompanied by a handwritten note — helped to humanize the war for both navy personnel and civilians.

While knitting and building their care packages, civilians often pictured the intended recipient as someone like Doug McCarthy — a considerate and decent human being who was serving his country. Although the war would destroy many of these men's lives and characters, McCarthy would remain a sensitive, kind man, thanks in part to the care and support of those at home.

Signing up blindly

McCarthy's character was developed early while on trips to the Christie Street Military Hospital in Toronto. Visiting his father's veteran friends taught the youngster patience. Sitting by an injured man's bedside, he learned of mustard gas, trench warfare, and other horrors of World War I. The sight of so many incapacitated, good men, missing their limbs or eyesight, deeply affected McCarthy. It was no wonder that he joined the Second Battalion of the Toronto Scottish Army Reserves while still a teenager.

With the onset of World War II coinciding with McCarthy's age for the military draft, his mother was naturally worried about the dangers in the army. But since there were many Toronto Maple Leaf hockey players in his reserve battalion, she heard that it was unlikely to be mobilized. Young McCarthy had to watch and wait as his older friends enlisted in all branches of the services to do their part.

When McCarthy came of age, he tried out for the air force but was turned down due to poor eyesight. Hearing rumours that the navy sometimes accepted vision-impaired recruits, McCarthy found out about a navy technical course that was looking for high school trainees.

But McCarthy still had to pass the medical examination. Halfway through the eye test, the doctor left the room to take a telephone call. When he returned, he signed McCarthy "OK" to enlist as an ordinary seaman. As a seaman, McCarthy was not permitted to wear glasses, yet he couldn't read a book without them. He was in the navy but life at sea would be challenging indeed!

Corvette duty

After training and qualifying as an Allied anti-submarine detection (asdic) operator, McCarthy was promoted to the navy's first recognized rank — able seaman. He could now apply a single chevron (V-stripe) to his new uniform. He was assigned to a corvette that escorted convoys sailing the Triangle Run between Newfoundland, New York, and Halifax.

On his first day, McCarthy stood on the deck of the corvette, breathing deeply, trying to settle his queasy stomach. Corvettes were notoriously buoyant ships: they rolled and pitched violently. McCarthy, like many first-time sailors, had difficulty adjusting to the motion.

Sailing up the St. Lawrence River, McCarthy tried to distract himself with what he could see of the passing scenery. "It'd be a lovely summer evening and the sun starting to fade on the hills." But then he'd have to leave the beauty behind to report for duty. He manned his equipment from the centre of the bridge, and it demanded his complete attention. His consolation: as a working location on the notoriously uncomfortable corvettes, the bridge was comparative luxury — "a nice, enclosed cabin."

McCarthy's seasickness would lessen over time. His ship was soon assigned to escort merchant ships in convoys from Halifax to the Western Ocean Meeting Place, 300 nautical miles off Newfoundland on the way to Britain. By staying long weeks at sea and not spending time on land, McCarthy found that his ability to handle the ship's motion improved.

McCarthy's corvette was expected to protect the convoy from submarines and surface enemies. His ship zigzagged, weaving back and forth alongside the merchant ships. This made it difficult for a submarine to mark the ship's position. For about five minutes, he and the other escorts would sail in one direction, and for the next five, in a different direction. The merchant ships, in the core of the convoy, continued to sail in line. Each ship had a dim light on the aft for the ship behind to follow, but it was barely visible in good weather and often not seen at all in bad conditions, adding to the many dangers of convoy travel.

Sub hunting

McCarthy's job on the corvette was to search for subs lurking around the convoy. His asdic machine was a 360-degree compass about 46 centimetres in diameter. It was connected to a big round oscillator sticking out from the bottom of the ship. "The equipment was basically underwater radar," he explains, an early form of sonar.

The day before the convoy sailed, the convoy masters were given information and instructions to determine the asdic sweep positions. The officer in charge then gave McCarthy the boundaries of the sweep.

"So you're doing this sweep, you move the equipment 5 degrees. It's a beam that goes out and is good to about 2,000 yards or so, and if it hasn't hit anything you move it 5 degrees, and then it sends the beam out again, and you move it another 5 degrees. You do this through the whole 45 degrees at 5 degree intervals." Sweeping was important and technical work, but it was probably as tedious as swabbing the decks.

Listening to the information from his equipment, McCarthy again had to sit quietly for long periods of time, day in and day out. Whenever an echo did come back, his heart skipped a beat. He would deftly guide the equipment to establish the length of the object, and if it looked suspicious, he turned on a recording device sitting beside the compass. Then he notified the officer of the watch.

If the image hadn't moved, the officer might declare it just another wreck. But when the feedback was suspicious, he promptly rang the action station's bell and the Higher Submarine Detector took over McCarthy's equipment. The ship also signalled to another vessel in the convoy, requesting assistance. It was time to attack — bring in the depth charges!

A depth charge was about the size of a large garbage pail with a potent explosive in its centre. The corvette had four "throwers" to send depth charges over the side. McCarthy set the depth charges at his station to explode at a specific depth, where the water pressure caused them to explode. If, as intended, the explosion's shock wave hit the hull of the submarine, it compromised the sub's watertight integrity. The sub's crew would be forced to bring the damaged vessel to the surface and, with any luck, surrender.

Dropping depth charges incurred a lot of danger. The second ship had to listen and maintain contact with the culprit because the attacker's asdic was usually knocked out. The corvettes travelled at a speed of only 15 nautical miles per hour full out, which meant that after dropping the depth charge, they were usually close to the explosion — especially if it occurred close to the surface of the water. "It was quite a shock to the ship," recalls McCarthy.

Unusual enemies

The dangers McCarthy encountered were not limited to submarines, especially once he was assigned to escort trans-Atlantic convoys. On one trip, McCarthy's ship travelled northwest for seven days, ending up among the ice floes of the North Atlantic. The men debated — only half in jest — where they'd be safest if attacked. "In among the ice floes there was no point in getting into a lifeboat," says McCarthy. The coldness of the air and water was sufficient to drain a person's body heat in minutes. McCarthy decided he would choose to go down in the boiler room. "At least with the guys down there, I'd be warm," he says.

Sailors also huddled in the bathroom area, below a

heavy leaded section that they believed would protect them from arms fire. Ironically, it was there that McCarthy discovered another enemy.

Submerged icebergs, capable of puncturing the ship's hull, made surface navigation hazardous. Collisions with icebergs, visible or invisible, or damage from capsizing icebergs also seriously threatened the low-lying corvette. A few inches of slush could even stall a freighter.

McCarthy one day watched with relief as his corvette passed through some ice floes uneventfully. Then he felt the call of nature. "I went to sit down in the bathroom," he says. "The bathroom on a corvette was right on the side of the ship, up forward, and there was metal, not the thickness of your finger, between you and the water. Well, we hit pack ice," he recalls. "And I'm telling you, it sounded like something had chewed the whole bottom of the ship up." McCarthy bolted out of the toilet as if he'd been fired like a rocket.

Captain in control

Despite the hazards, McCarthy and his fellow seamen generally had faith in their captain and senior officers. "We were convinced it wouldn't be our ship that would get hit," he says. "We always felt the captain would know what to do to keep us safe."

And their trust was not misplaced. One morning when McCarthy's ship, the *Summerside*, was sailing in the war zone of the Mediterranean, McCarthy woke up and looked out at the convoy. The freighters were missing their barrage balloons! Barrage balloons were small balloons attached to support wires or nets that were used as protection against air attacks. The balloons would deceive the radar of incoming planes. "They were all gone that morning as we made our way to Gibraltar," McCarthy says. Rather than unnerve the men, McCarthy's discovery only reinforced their faith in their captain. "When the balloons had been knocked off, the captain was on the loud hailer giving instructions to change course and do this, and do that. You'd have thought it was Foster Hewitt doing a game from Maple Leaf Gardens," says McCarthy.

Once a navigating officer on a Bermuda tourist ship, this particular captain never trusted the bearings he was given, says McCarthy. He took his own readings and made his own calculations. Despite the navigational resources of the escorted convoy, the captain always knew his own ship's exact location. If fog closed in, he needed to know quickly what his position was.

Once, en route to Londonderry, Ireland, in a convoy, the captain's rescue ship was detailed to stay with a stricken oil tanker while the rest of the convoy sped on. After picking up survivors in the middle of nowhere, the captain had to lay out a course, quickly get away from the area, and catch up to the convoy. Not a problem for this experienced seaman.

Alas, not everyone appreciated the captain's superior skills. One day, off the coast of foggy Newfoundland, the

Summerside was trying to locate the position of an elusive convoy. "You'd think it would be easy to locate a group of 40 to 60 ships out in the ocean, but you could be behind them and they've gone on to New York and you ain't going to catch up to it for a long time," laughs McCarthy. Commander Prentice, light reflecting off his numerous gold braids, was aboard another of the searching vessels. He outranked the other ships' captains, who were mere navy lieutenants. After much time had passed without success, McCarthy's captain recommended a specific change of course, likely correct, but not well received by the commander.

TLC

McCarthy was grateful for the captain's seafaring skills, as well as his other demonstrations of care. McCarthy, for one, never completely got over being seasick. Sometimes he was ill on board, and if he was on land leave for long, he'd feel unwell upon returning to the ship. "I wasn't sick like some of them, though," he says empathetically. The *Summerside* captain always came through for the worse-off, letting them off at the next harbour. "I guess it was good thinking," says McCarthy, who knew from experience. "They weren't of any use while they were in that shape."

It was actually the noise of the ocean, as well as the noises within the ship, that unsettled McCarthy the most. "The seaman's mess deck was right up near the sharp end you see," he says. "There were two anchor cables that went down through to the chain locker, and when it was rough, those bang-banged." Later in the war, ships' cables were tied down so that they didn't slam about, but that improvement came too late for McCarthy's benefit. The howling wind also caused the funnel of the ship to moan, and the *slam-slosh* noise of the waves as they crashed down all contributed to McCarthy's motion sickness. Despite it, McCarthy never missed being on watch. Often he felt better on deck.

McCarthy's captain tried to make the gruelling journeys easier on his wartime crew in other ways. At Christmas, when the ship reached harbour, the officers served the men dinner. The youngest sailor on the ship, Glenn Waddy, was declared captain for the day. As was the prerogative of the captain, Waddy "spliced the main brace" for double issues of rum. He did this three times. Each time, McCarthy would escort Waddy to the captain to get the keys to open the rum compartment. "The captain, he wasn't feeling any pain either," laughs McCarthy. "He handed him the keys and said, 'Your power's waning, Waddy, your power's waning!'"

Mail arrived sporadically but when it did, it also helped to relieve the men's seasickness and homesickness. Whenever McCarthy received a personal package containing cocoa or some other delicacy, he always brought it out of his locker and shared it with the men who were about to go on the 1600 watch. "At four o'clock you went out for two hours and didn't get supper until after the watch, so you were pretty hungry," he says. McCarthy's kindness was appreciated, particularly after the men had been at sea more than a couple of days. "[By] then the ship's menu changed considerably," says McCarthy. "There was no fresh milk or fresh fruit." McCarthy's tokens were considered a real treat.

Gut-wrench time

But the camaraderie and kindness of sailors offered only limited protection when the horrors of war struck. One of McCarthy's worst naval experiences was on a convoy numbered HX212. It was a fast convoy that left Newfoundland at the end of October 1941, bound for Londonderry. This time, McCarthy was aboard one of the convoy's rescue ships. "The first two nights were quiet. And then they were ready for us," he says.

Enemy subs torpedoed one of the convoy's tankers, but the main convoy had to continue on regardless. In the event of attack, the convoy was always supposed to get away from the danger as quickly as possible. It was a fact of naval life that saving men's lives was secondary to protecting the cargo. But McCarthy's ship stayed behind, specifically tasked with finding and rescuing any convoy sailors in the water. As the ship hung around the blazing tanker, "The captain, with his good seamanship, manoeuvred in as close as he could [despite] the burning oil in the water," says McCarthy.

Lowering scramble nets over the side of their ship, McCarthy and the crew tried to save who they could. Men floundering in the water grabbed desperately for the nets and tried to climb up the rocking, heaving ship. McCarthy watched as his shipmates leaned over the side as far as they could, extending their arms to help haul the sailors aboard. "You felt for the guys. They were covered with oil and grease and stuff, and they're hard to get a hold of, and they can't breathe that well because they've got that stuff up their noses and in their mouths."

The ship rose and fell in the waves like a cork. "It was quite difficult because one moment they'd be down there, and the next they'd be up maybe 20 feet because of the sea." The captain apologized, because he couldn't go any slower or stop; he didn't know if there were still submarines in the area. "It was scary," recalls McCarthy. "The tanker was hit, on blazing fire, these men are in the ocean, nobody knows how many were in there ... And a lot of these men couldn't swim."

They saved about 10 or 12 men, McCarthy guesses, but eventually, even his rescue ship was ordered to move on. Despite the convoy's efforts to make haste and stay out of trouble, it had again come under attack. McCarthy's rescue ship had to do what it could once more.

This was a gut-wrenching time for McCarthy, no doubt equal to the horrific stories of World War I he used to hear at the vets' hospital. Freezing, frightened sailors — many just teenagers — watched as McCarthy's rescue ship revved up and sailed away, leaving them surrounded by miles and miles of deep, cold, heaving water. In his characteristic understatement, McCarthy says, "It wasn't a very pleasant part of the operation."

Fortunately the abandoned sailors had life jackets to keep them afloat and preserve core body heat. McCarthy hoped that when the two corvettes farther back in the convoy reached the men's vicinity, they might be better positioned to take the time to fish the rest out of the water. He worried that the sailors, in their dismay and fear, may not have understood there was more help coming.

Hide the Easter eggs

It was especially after such unsettling horror that the thoughtfulness and caring words of people who sent care packages had the most impact. McCarthy left with yet another convoy from Londonderry in October and didn't get any mail until some time in February. A ship from Britain, going to Gibraltar, had some extra space that was filled with mail. "It was a bonanza," says McCarthy of the mail. "*Toronto Daily Stars* from home, mail, and these gift packages!" The packages helped to remind them that their dangerous work during the war was appreciated.

McCarthy considered himself one of the most fortunate. He was on the "care" list of both his public school and high school, and two churches. "So I got all kinds of things," he says. The sailors shared their spoils with one another. What one man didn't like, another man did. "The only thing I drew a line on was Laura Secord Easter eggs," says McCarthy. He surreptitiously hid them in his locker. "I might go on watch at two o'clock in the morning when no one was around, and then I'd help myself to my Easter eggs!"

By 1943, McCarthy began to wonder how much damage he was doing to his eyes by not wearing glasses. "I'd had a lot of time to think and it looked like the war was going to go on for a long time," he says. He decided to pursue other work in the navy, work that would permit him to wear glasses. Transferring out of asdic, he became a coder in communications for the last two years of the war.

Long after the war had ended, McCarthy came full circle. As he had once learned about war from hospitalized military veterans, he too shared his wartime experiences as a veteran. Instead of making a statement with a broken body, McCarthy enlisted naval photos, maps, and diagrams. In his gentle, patient way, he described and interpreted the war for children who found its horrors hard to imagine.

Chapter 2
The Most Heavily Attacked Convoy in the War

Joe Marston (late) [Merchant Navy and Royal Canadian Navy]

Born on the west coast with an appreciation of all things nautical, Joe Marston seemed destined for adventures at sea. As a youngster, he had watched the ships coming and going from the Vancouver harbour. Joining the Canadian Sea Cadets, he learned responsibility, leadership, and other valuable qualities that would prove useful later in life. Revering all the tools of a seaman — uniform, telescope, and Abney level (a nautical surveying instrument) — Marston joined the merchant navy as a bridge messenger at the young age of 16.

Marston loved nothing more than having a ship under

his feet. By 24 years of age, he had left one coast of Canada for the other to sail with the famous Atlantic convoy SC7. It provided him with some amazing war adventures — even before he transferred over to the Canadian Navy.

SC7 departs

At noon on October 5, 1940, the convoy SC7 sailed out of Sydney, Nova Scotia, bound for Britain. Among the 39 small, mostly old and heavily loaded ships was the SS *Blairspey*, carrying a full load of cargo. Joe Marston was second mate.

By dark, the ships had formed into nine columns with four ships in each, plus one column of three ships. Each column was about 900 metres apart, and ships in the column were about 550 metres yards apart. The convoy speed was seven knots.

Because the less time a convoy spent crossing the ocean, the less likely it was to be detected by U-boats, a two-speed system had been devised for convoys — fast and slow. Fast convoys sailed at about nine knots, slow ones at about seven knots. The difference in speed made about three days difference in the length of time it took to cross the Atlantic.

To protect Marston's convoy in its crossing, the navy had provided two ocean escort ships. The HMS *Scarborough* was a 1000-ton sloop equipped with an early-type sonar, a four-inch low-angle gun, and a few light anti-aircraft weapons. The HMCS *Elk*, an armed yacht, remained with the convoy for only a day. A light Royal Canadian Air Force (RCAF) aircraft was assigned to patrol in the convoy's vicinity during daylight hours, until dark of the second day. After that, the ships were on their own.

Soon after the convoy got under way, the crews were ordered to practise emergency procedures, including signalling, turning, and manning their action stations. They already had to contend with the horrific Atlantic weather. An experienced naval man, Marston could sense that this crossing was not going to be easy.

The dangers of straggling

The convoy was an unusual group of vessels. "Most were coal burners, which meant uneven speeds, black smoke, and difficult station keeping, particularly at the change of watch, when ashes and clinkers were drawn from the furnaces," says Marston. One ship soon developed generator problems and returned to Sydney. The following day, another ship, the *Shekateka*, joined the convoy. Unable to keep up with the convoy she had originally sailed with, and fearful of her vulnerability as a lone ship, her crew was glad to find and join SC7. But safety in a convoy was never guaranteed.

The gale-force winds and heavy seas had caused four ships to straggle from the convoy. One ship was able to catch up and rejoin the convoy, but another reported that she had been torpedoed and was sinking. Seven of her 21 crew members had been killed.

Soon afterward, the *Aneos* was hit, too. The *Eaglecliffe*

Hall, coming up astern, picked up the crew. Unescorted, it made its way safely to the River Clyde in Scotland, although it had been heading for Preston, England.

Despite all these early troubles to its straggling ships, the main convoy had not yet reached the area of the Atlantic that was designated "U-boat Danger Zone"— east of longitude 210° west. Later in the war, the entire Atlantic Ocean was considered a danger zone.

At dusk, 12 days after departure, the *Scarborough's* sister ship, the HMS *Fowey,* and the brand-new corvette HMS *Bluebell* joined the convoy to offer additional protection. Few of the merchant ships had seen them approaching in the dark. Were there more vessels out there they were also unaware of?

First attack

In good weather and under a nearly full moon, the main convoy suffered its first double attack on October 17. This time, Marston and the *Blairspey* found themselves in the middle of all the action.

The *Languedoc,* sailing behind the *Blairspey,* and the *Scoresby,* on its starboard beam, were torpedoed simultaneously. "There was no need to sound any alarms as the explosions and shock waves had people running from all points," says Marston.

By light and sound signal, the commodore altered the convoy's course 40 degrees to starboard. Then it had to continue, leaving just the rescue ship *Bluebell* to pick up survivors. On the *Blairspey*, Marston's and the other sailors' hearts were beating a little faster.

Loss of escort vessels made the crews more anxious. Aided by a Sunderland aircraft from the Coastal Command, the *Scarborough* and its sister ship hunted for the culprit U-boat relentlessly. "The convoy was sans escort until the afternoon," says Marston. "Although it kept the U-boat submerged, it had no success with depth charges. The *Scarborough* fell far behind and at her best speed, 14 knots, never did regain the convoy." Not only did the *Scarborough's* absence weaken the convoy's defence in the event of an attack, it increased its own vulnerability as a lone ship in the middle of the ocean.

Quite unexpectedly — but fortunately — two other escort ships joined the convoy: the HMS *Leith* and the HMS *Heartease*. No sooner had they taken their positions than one of the merchant ships, the *Carsbreck*, was attacked. The debilitated ship was stricken on her port side forward. She was only able to proceed at the slow speed of six knots. The *Heartease* escorted her to the River Clyde.

The main convoy now forged ahead with three escorts. The *Blairspey* was unscathed, but Marston was on the look-out for more trouble. Convoy ships were not to wait for the commodore's orders when spotting torpedoes or approaching an enemy, but to immediately signal to the convoy to turn away from the danger. This rule would save many lives.

About half an hour after the *Carsbreck* was hit, Marston was on his watch on the bridge. His lookout reported two torpedoes passing ahead of the convoy from port to starboard. "I immediately sounded the alarm, plugged in the green light, and sounded one short blast on the ship's whistle," Marston says. At this signal, the whole convoy automatically altered course to the predetermined 40 degrees to the starboard side.

Official sources credit the commodore's ship with giving the signal, but when the commodore's ship signalled *Blairspey* by light the next day, asking if she had given the warning, "the modest reply was 'yes,'" says Marston. He had saved the day — at least for the time being.

Marston turned in fully clothed at 1900 that night. It had been a hectic day and he was on the middle watch, which always came around too early. "At 2015, I heard the ominous and frightening booms and felt the shock waves of ships being torpedoed and blown up on the starboard side of the convoy," says Marston. "Another and another explosion occurred, more than any I had ever known."

For the next few hours, the ship experienced more explosions and shock waves. Then "the torpedo with our name on it smashed into the forward port side just below the foremast," says Marston. "When the smoke cleared and the shudders ceased, most of the deck cargo of lumber was angled up around the mast like an Indian teepee."

Marston ran to the bridge to ensure that his senior

officers were all right. Not only was he concerned about their welfare, he was next in command. "Both Captain Jimmy Walker and First Mate John Glasgow were most competent and well-liked, and always kept their heads no matter what," says Marston. The captain ordered Marston and the third mate to go to the boat deck and calm the men. Then they were to rehoist the starboard lifeboat that had been dropped by three panicky sailors.

Fortunately, the generator was still functioning. The lifeboat had swung around and was being towed stern first, banging against the ship's side. Marston couldn't turn the boat even with help. With a struggle, and the help of a generator, they hoisted it stern to ship's bow until it reached the davit heads, the projection over the side of the ship used to hold lifeboats.

Marston went down to the engine room, where the two Scottish engineers were working bravely and furiously to get the engines running again. Joints in the lines that carried steam from boilers to the main engine had been damaged. They had to be wrenched up or repacked before steam could be applied to the engine. Marston tried to help them, but after a few minutes, he was unable to get the thought of a torpedo crashing through the thin steel hull plates out of his mind. With arms weak from fear, he realized he wasn't helping much, so he left the engineers to it. His premonitions came true a little while later.

The torpedoes kept coming

"At about midnight, another torpedo struck forward, again just below the foremast, but this time on the starboard side, directly opposite the first," says Marston. The captain ordered the lifeboats to be lowered and manned, but to remain close to the damaged *Blairspey* until daylight, when they would board again and try to get her to Britain.

Everyone prepared to abandon ship. Secret books containing information on codes, destinations, and other information that shouldn't get into enemy hands were dumped overboard in a weighted bag.

Like every sailor, Marston knew to take along only what was most precious to him. "I had my brand-new sextant complete with mahogany box in my grip. It cost me two months' pay," says Marston. "Then the captain handed me a case containing the ship's papers and his own 'slop chest,' and accounts. The canny Scottish captain made sure to take his accounting information! So I just set the sextant down on the starboard bridge wing and walked to the lifeboat," says Marston.

"The boat was already waterborne, and just as we were about to go down the ladder, apprentice Jim McMenamin grabbed my arm and said, 'Look — a submarine!' Sure enough, across the stern was a fully surfaced U-boat standing out in sharp relief in the full moon," says Marston.

The captain told Marston quietly, "Man the gun." Marston quickly led his gun crew across the afterdeck, over the cargo, and onto the poop deck platform. Determined to avenge the damage to his ship, Marston grabbed the weapon. It had a shell and a charge of cordite in the breach, but no detonator. His heart sunk in dismay.

The U-boat escaped into the darkness. The *Blairspey* was threatening to submerge. While the gun crew slid down the grab lines at breakneck speed, the captain and chief steward made a more dignified descent down the ladder into the lifeboat.

Incredibly, the moment they landed in the boat, a third torpedo struck below the bridge on the port side. "There were the usual shudders, loud explosion, and this time much smoke, soot, and flames shooting from the funnel," says Marston. "Lumber was flying everywhere but we were shielded by the ship's side above us. However, a deluge of water showered down into the boat, half filling it and soaking all hands."

Blairspey was threatening to break in two and sink. "The boiler room and engine room must surely have been filled with water, and while the lumber cargo might support her — on our previous crossing we had been carrying steel — it was obvious that without power we could not sail her home," says Marston.

The crew, now bailing water out of lifeboats, began to put distance between themselves and their ship. If the *Blairspey* were to sink, it could pull their lifeboat under the water. "We set off for bonnie Scotland about 200 miles down the road," says Marston. "It was cold and wet and uncomfortable, but we were happy to be alive and the weather was not too bad ... yet."

Errands of mercy

Hours later, a dark shape loomed up alongside the lifeboats. Alarmed at what they thought was another U-boat, the men were relieved to discover it was the convoy's own HMS *Bluebell*. "Still on her errands of mercy," says Marston, remembering his gratefulness. "By timing our leaps to the seas, we could jump onto the rescue ship's deck."

"The *Bluebell* already had hundreds of survivors aboard, and in the ensuing hours, she picked up more — bringing the total number to more than 300, in addition to 60 of her own crew. Despite the intense crowding on the ship, very little food supplies, and the rising wind and sea, the rescued men were in lively and good spirits," says Marston. "This was better than *Blairspey's* lifeboat by far."

While Marston was counting his blessings, other crew members had run into more trouble. Although everyone had seen First Mate Glasgow taking charge of the portside lifeboat, they were unaware that he and his crew had difficulty getting the lifeboat into the water. A torpedo struck just forward of Glasgow's boat when it was no more than a metre from the ship's side. The lifeboat was flung on its end, dumping some of the men into the sea.

They spent the night anchored at sea, and the following

day, they saw a Sunderland aircraft of the Coastal Command circling them. The aircraft didn't see them, but the crew pulled back toward the *Blairspey* anyway. Glasgow assumed, correctly, that the aircraft would inform shore authorities of the wreck, and they would direct a tug to it. The tug, *Salvania*, arrived in time to rescue the men before dark, but they had to wait for daylight for the chance to secure a towline.

In the morning, Glasgow and his men were able to reboard the *Blairspey*. They rounded up some stores, such as cigarettes, for the tug, and then secured the heavy towline around the after poop deckhouse. "She could not be towed from forward because her shattered fore section was now only hinged to the after part. And so the *Blairspey* was towed drunkenly, after end first, all the way to Scotland's River Clyde," says Marston. Before the trip was over, the *Salvania* had picked up another 100 survivors from five other ships in the convoy. SC7 went down in history as the most attacked convoy in the war.

A few days later, Marston and Glasgow went to look at the badly beaten *Blairspey*. "Engine and boiler rooms and all the forward section were flooded," reports Marston. "The forward deck cargo had disappeared, washed overboard. The bridge house containing the deck officers' accommodations had been shifted about six feet to port, and officers' rooms and the dining saloon were unrecognizable.

"A bus could be driven through each of the three holes in the ship's side made by the torpedoes. But there, in spite of all the mayhem, resting unscathed on the deck of the starboard bridge was my precious sextant exactly as I had left it," he says. The sextant continued to serve the professional seaman well after the war.

Chapter 3
Of Ships and Tanks

Jim McParlan
[Royal Canadian Navy RCNVR V32691]

hen men went off to war, they had no idea how disagreeable their working conditions would be nor how they'd react to contact with the enemy. Some men withered, some did what they were told to do, while others excelled and performed amazing feats. Few men, especially in the navy, can claim to have lassoed a tank. But Jim McParlan brought one to a complete stop using only his bare hands.

In April 1941, the decision for the teenaged McParlan to join the navy was simple. "When I saw all my buddies going in the navy, I had to go in the navy, too," he says. But instead of sailing away with camaraderie and comfort, he found himself entrenched in dirty work, sometimes meeting up with dirty characters, and definitely fighting in a dirty war.

Dirty jobs

Like all new recruits, McParlan undertook basic training and then was assigned to nethermost work. "I climbed inside the boiler and cleaned the soot," he says. "It was particularly difficult in mine sweepers because they're so small you had to lie on your back to scrape them off." And it was especially uncomfortable for McParlan, who stood six feet tall.

After almost a year and a half of cleaning boilers, McParlan was eager to find cleaner, more comfortable work. He was sent to Toronto to take a course on maintaining small engines of landing craft. He thought he'd left the dirty jobs behind.

After completing the course, and with the war heating up, McParlan anticipated that he'd be sent overseas right away. Instead, he was sent to Newfoundland. From Newfoundland, McParlan sailed to Halifax, where he boarded the SS *Louis Pasteur*, a ship with an interesting background. A luxury liner of impressive speed, on her maiden voyage, the *Louis Pasteur* raced across the Atlantic to deliver more than 193 tonnes of gold bullion to Canada for safekeeping, thus saving France's gold reserves. Now, with McParlan aboard, the *Louis Pasteur* was joining a convoy to ferry troops to Europe.

"Whenever we were travelling over the sea, we travelled

in convoy," says McParlan. "I went over to England from Halifax on the *Louis Pasteur,* and we were only one of many, many ships." Each ship had a strategic position within the convoy. In the middle of the convoy — better protected from torpedoes — were vessels carrying explosives or highly flammable cargo. Ships on the outside of the convoy were more likely to be hit by German U-boats attacking head-on, so they carried less volatile cargo, such as grain or lumber. Escort ships flanked the outside edges of the vessels. By 1941, rescue ships had been added to the basic convoy composition. Before then, when escorts went to pick up survivors from torpedoed vessels, they left the convoy unprotected.

The *Louis Pasteur* was vigorously protected because of its valuable cargo. On board, "we were just a bunch of young sailors going to Greenock, Scotland," says McParlan. Other than being put to work once in a while, there was little for any of the men to do. They played cards, talked to one another, and endured monumental boredom. "We were really travelling as passengers," says McParlan. The troops did wonder about what they would do on the other side of the Atlantic. They correctly believed it would involve landing craft and invasions — what was known as combined operations.

Combined ops

Most of McParlan's seafaring time from then on was spent in combined ops, manoeuvres that involved the joint efforts of Allied navy, army, and air forces. In June 1943, McParlan sailed with the 55th Canadian Landing Craft Assault flotilla for the Mediterranean.

While waiting in the North African port of Mers-el-Kabir for the invasion of Sicily to begin, they had to do unfamiliar physical exercises, marching 8 or 10 kilometres in a day, as well as doing push-ups on the ship. The invasion was one of the largest combined operations of the war. Half a million Allied servicemen fought for control of the island. When they succeeded, Sicily became a base for the invasion of Italy as well as a training ground for Allied troops who would land on the beaches of Normandy 11 months later.

"After Sicily, we went back to Salerno to get ready for Operation Avalanche on September 9, 1942," McParlan says. "It was a typical invasion, very bad. We had to do a second landing with reinforcements to get inland." Leaving the mother ship, the *Otranto,* McParlan's small landing craft carried about three dozen soldiers plus three crew: the stoker, coxswain, and seaman. It took about 10 minutes to get the men from the ship to the beach and another 20 minutes to unload them.

As the stoker on the craft, McParlan worked nonstop at the stern of the vessel. Sitting between two engines, he watched a telegraph with the speeds indicated on it. Whatever message was conveyed on the telegraph, McParlan had to deliver that speed.

McParlan was below deck, and alone. The space was so crammed that he couldn't stand upright unless he opened the hatch. There was lots of noise outside during the landing. "But I felt safe that the engines were somewhat protective," he says, adding, "It's a wonder they didn't deafen me." Although each individual trip might take close to an hour, McParlan made continuous trips throughout the day, going back and forth to the *Otranto*. When his vessel was at rest, he changed oil filters or cleaned the gasoline engines. Once again he was doing the dirty, but necessary, work of the navy.

First Canadian
Next McParlan was sent to Portsmouth to receive training in preparation for landing in France. It was here that he had one of his cleaner assignments, but it was also during this period that the term "dirty, rotten scoundrels" may have been born.

"My job on the *Resolution*, while she was being conditioned for the invasion, was guarding the cells of the battleship," says McParlan. In the cells was a Canadian from Peterborough. "I considered myself responsible for the Canadian only," he says. "I was also responsible, as I found out later, for the RN guys who were in cells, as well." One of these Royal Navy (RN) men escaped during McParlan's watch and went home to Glasgow. He was quickly caught and returned to the ship by military policemen. But because McParlan was on duty at the time, McParlan was also charged. "I got 30 days stoppage of leave." McParlan wasn't at all happy about this but felt he got some sweet revenge. "I used to sneak out of the barracks at night, and over the bridge, and into the town of Shirley there, then into a local hotel, and nobody knew I was gone," he says.

When McParlan's landing craft for France — a much bigger vessel than his previous landing craft — arrived in Portsmouth, he became a crew member of the 260th Canadian Landing Craft Infantry Large, designated the First Canadian.

Preparation for the top-secret amphibious invasion of the continent was being stepped up, though the sailors didn't know exactly when it would take place. The sailors left from the docks through the East Solent. D-day was cancelled on June 5, due to bad weather, but that evening, McParlan and company moved from their position off the Isle of Wight and headed out into the channel towards Normandy. With thousands of other ships, they arrived near France's famous beach at 0600.

Rope tricks

McParlan's job was to take the lifeline, attached to the ramp of the landing craft, and wade ashore. The line was a strong coconut rope, about five centimetres in diameter, that floated on water. "I had the coiled rope over my shoulders," he says. He swam in water about two metres deep, until his feet touched bottom. As he waded towards land, he prayed silently. "I wasn't so worried about myself," he says. "I was thinking about my poor mother. She's going to be really sad when she gets the telegram telling her I've been killed."

McParlan dragged the line and himself onto the beach. He dug his heels into the sand and pulled the line taut, holding it with both hands so that the soldiers had something to hang on to as they waded to shore. Once ashore, McParlan was supposed to coil the lifeline. "I was supposed to get inside that coil of rope to protect me. Imagine!" he says.

But when he reached the beach, there was so much commotion, gunfire, and shouting, he was unable to concentrate on coiling the rope. He threw the line out behind himself rather than coiling it. "A British tank ran over the damned line," he says. "The rope got in its tank treads and it pulled me over, and I thought 'Oh Christ, I've been shot for sure,' as the damned tank was pulling me along the beach."

It pulled him for about three metres. A British Army sergeant running beside the tank shouted "Stop! Stop! Stop!" and hammered on the side of the tank. The tank finally stopped. "If he'd kept going, he'd have dragged me and dragged my landing craft, too," recalls McParlan. "They probably would've snapped the rope and God knows the chaos," he says. As it was, the sergeant couldn't get the rope out of the treads, so he pulled out his knife and cut it. "Oh, what a relief that was!"

McParlan could still hear the bullets zinging past him as he went back to his position and waited for the craft to unload. Once the last soldier was unloaded, he returned to the landing craft. The tide had receded, and the water was now only up to his knees. Wading through the murky water, what McParlan found most unnerving was the possibility of being shot by a sniper. This was another tough assignment for McParlan.

The landing craft then returned to England to get another 150 or so troops to transport. "We had to make numerous trips over the next few months," he says. McParlan repeated his rope tricks, minus the escapade with the tank.

McParlan started the war off tough on soot and grime, but later, leading the troops off his landing craft in Normandy, he demonstrated the true grit required of Canadian seamen. His deeds were the stuff of which movies are made.

Chapter 4
The Prayers of War
Arthur Hadley [Royal Canadian Navy Escort Group C-7]

F aith can play an important role in times of war. Men who never give a second thought to spiritual matters in peacetime often turn to religion or spiritual colleagues for comfort during war. Arthur Hadley was already a spiritual man, but two years of service in wartime sealed his faith and his destiny.

Like many young boys, Arthur Hadley showed a keen interest in airplanes. However, at 13 years old, he went aboard a couple of navy ships docked near his home in Halifax, Nova Scotia. After this, his aeronautical interest was superceded by a love of ships. Even with his new love of seagoing vessels,

Hadley didn't expect to become a sailor. He believed his real destiny was the Baptist ministry. But it's often said that God works in mysterious ways, and Hadley was to find goodness, as well as glimpses of Hell, as a wartime sailor.

Father leads the way

Before Hadley made it to sea, his father, approaching 40 years of age, enlisted in the army. When the war first broke out, he decided that nobody else should be responsible for his family. He was sent overseas with a hospital unit in 1941. At 16, too young to join up, Hadley watched in fascination as his father — and the first naval destroyers — left Halifax to help Britain in the war. As the battleships sailed out to escort the troop ships in convoys, Hadley had only an inkling of the dangers they faced.

While his father was at war, Hadley and his mother moved to a Baptist parsonage. In his father's absence, young Hadley looked to the minister, originally from Lancashire, England, for guidance. Sometimes the minister made an impression in unexpected ways. "The weekend that the *Bismarck* sunk the *Hood* and looked like it was going to destroy convoys, that minister was just glued to the radio," Hadley says.

The following year, Hadley wrote his father for permission to join the navy. His father replied, "For your mother's sake, wait until your 18th birthday." Less than a year later, his father sent him $10 — a substantial sum in those days — and asked him to take his mother out to celebrate their wedding anniversary and Hadley's 18th birthday. As they finished supper, without any reference to the topic of enlistment, his mother said, "I'll just catch a streetcar and go home if you want to go over to the navy office tonight." Hadley had just started dating a girl named Edna, but that night, October 25, 1943, he enlisted in the Royal Canadian Navy.

The enlisting officer asked Hadley if he was mechanically inclined. "No," he replied candidly. Demonstrating the practicality of sailors, the officer said, "Then you'd best stay out of gunnery." Hadley happily agreed. Soon, he was sent for four weeks of basic training and six weeks on the HMCS *Cornwallis*, with a 20-week course at signal school. Hadley learned to use a 10-inch signal lamp (or Aldis lamp) to send Morse code. Twenty-two men started the course, 16 took the final exam, and only half of them passed.

His job as a signalman in the navy was to relay communications between the ships of a convoy. "Occasionally, if a ship was on the horizon, we would send messages by a 20-inch searchlight with a shutter," he says. Not everybody could read messages from that far away, but Hadley took pride in having exceptional eyesight. Hoping to unlock biblical messages for parishioners one day so that they could see the light, Hadley was now, ironically, sending and translating messages delivered by rays of light.

Assigned to a Montreal-built frigate, the *Lanark*, Hadley promptly sent his mother and Edna messages. "I sent them

An Aldis lamp

telegrams so they'd be conditioned to getting them," he says, alluding to the navy's method of notifying family members of the death or injury of their kin.

Comforts on board

On board the ship, Hadley made many friends. Some friendships blossomed from unexpected beginnings. In 1940, friends of his parents had built a hut to be used as a soldier's and airman's Christian association in Halifax. "My father and I put the first coat of paint on that hut," says Hadley. At the hut for a church service one Sunday evening, Hadley met a sailor, Norm Jolly, who told Hadley he was on the *Lanark*. "It didn't mean anything to me because I was still on the base," says Hadley. But once assigned to the *Lanark*, Hadley and Jolly found each other assigned to the same mess deck.

Hadley also became close friends with Bill Ruddy from Jasper, Alberta. They talked a lot about what they were going to do after the war, what university or college courses they'd take and where. Veterans were entitled to financial credits after the war to apply to their education, which otherwise they might not have been able to afford.

Little money was needed in the middle of the ocean. Staying warm and dry were the sailors' primary concerns. No one on board ships the size of the *Lanark*, a frigate, wore conventional navy uniforms. Instead, they wore caps or balaclavas and practical clothing. "It was cold at sea, so we wore duffle coats," says Hadley. Some men wore sea boots, or rubber boots. "I suffered from cold feet, so I'd bought a pair of flying boots, and I went on watch with my slippers on and fur-lined flying boots," says Hadley. "My feet were warm!" Woollen sweaters and blue jeans were the uniform of the sea. Only while leaving and entering harbour was dress uniform donned.

When not busy, Hadley was always happy to read or talk to the other sailors. "You'd talk about everything," he says. "My difficulty was, with my background, I couldn't stand the continual discussions of sex or the language always laced with blasphemy. But one thing I discovered — and I've always been glad I discovered it in the navy — was that guys can be good without being religious."

Hadley often slept on deck under the heavens. "We had slinging space for 18 hammocks in our mess deck and there were 28 of us in there," says Hadley. He was told that he could sleep on the lockers. "They had pads, you sat on them at the table, which was fine in port, but the first time I fell off in a heavy sea and hit a steel deck, I decided I would take those cushions and put them on the deck and sleep right down there."

Although Hadley's faith meant that he never lost sleep at night worrying about whether or not his ship would be torpedoed, others may have. "Some of them had difficulty sleeping, but they dealt with it," he says. "If they couldn't hack it, the navy sent them back to base."

On the North American side of the ocean, ships gathered in Boston, New York, and Halifax, for the Triangle Run. Escorts brought the ships from those three places and started across the Atlantic from south of Newfoundland. "Our group always sailed from St. John's, Newfoundland, and then we would take a convoy all the way to Britain," says Hadley.

Now he was a part of the important convoys he had seen his father leaving with, and he was the sailor he didn't think he'd be. "The interesting thing is, I couldn't swim, and still can't swim," he says. In fact, many young naval enlistees couldn't, and rushed efforts to teach recruits to stay afloat were inadequate anyway if a ship went down. "In the North Atlantic, you didn't have much of a chance," says Hadley. "There was so much power and strength at sea."

Unlike most, Hadley was never seasick. And although he didn't like the cold, he was content to be on deck when it was his turn to be on watch. He enjoyed it so much that when he got shore leave, he looked forward to getting back to his ship.

Periodically, Hadley and the crew of the *Lanark* were called to action stations, at which time they practised dropping depth charges. Otherwise their war was uneventful at first. Hadley spent a lot of time thinking about his family and life back home.

"I'd often be thinking about my dad because by the time I got to sea he was in France," says Hadley. "Mother was with her mother. I always looked forward to hitting port and getting my mail. People from my church would write me, my dad, my mother, my girlfriend. I was always interested to hear what was going on. The guys razzed me, but I never went ashore on the first night at port. I'd read all my letters and write back then."

Of course, Christmas Day was Hadley's favourite time aboard ship. In addition to the spiritual significance of the day, Hadley enjoyed the naval traditions. "The youngest person on board is captain for Christmas morning," he says. Since Hadley was second youngest, he became coxswain and donned the rotund coxswain's uniform. Since the real coxswain was always seen with a cigar, Hadley, despite detesting the habit, walked around with an unlit one protruding from his lips. The two officers-for-the-day had a blast. "Of course, we told the officers that the wardroom was a mess, and it needed to be cleaned up," says Hadley mischievously.

Runaway

It's often at such pleasant times that people let their guard down, and Hadley's was soon to be tested. While waiting in the harbour for their turn for repairs, the captain announced he was going ashore. Hadley, as duty signalman that day, was expected to accompany him. The motorboat was lowered, and Hadley got in with his signal flags, wet cell battery, and Aldis lamp. He sat there waiting for the captain and the stoker who would navigate the boat, only to be told that the plans had changed. The captain would not be going ashore until later. "I thought, well I'm not going to climb back up there with all this wet acid that can get all over my uniform. So I literally fell asleep with nothing to do," he says.

Suddenly, Hadley heard cries and woke up. "Some seaman did not tie the proper legal knot," he exclaimed, realizing his motorboat was heading out to sea in an outgoing tide without the benefit of a "qualified operator." At the mouth of the bay were anti-submarine apparatus that vessels had to zigzag around. Trying desperately to get the motorboat started, Hadley was unable to differentiate between the many knobs. "I got to the first of these barriers and I thought, I can't just hit this thing and smash up the boat, so I steered it around and then went back to trying to pull levers," he says. He got to the second one and did the same. The third one was the last obstacle on an outgoing tide. "I didn't have a life belt. I was heading out to sea!"

Finally, he stepped on something accidentally and discovered it was the starter. But the motorboat was in reverse. Once he was able to get the boat moving forward, he had to run back to the stern to steer. Eventually, he made his way back to the ship and the Jacob's ladder that was hanging over the side of the deck. Sailors, hanging over the ship's rails, urged him to come on under. Hadley cut the power and resumed steering. But alas, the little craft was still moving too fast.

"Steel hooks on the end of the Jacob's ladder got the top of the roof and just lifted it off," says Hadley. "If I hadn't ducked, I'd have been decapitated." He had to start the engine again, and this time the sailors urged him to come and nudge the stern. "I hit and bounced back," laughs Hadley. "Everybody's yelling at me." On the next try, he succeeded.

As he came aboard ship, the captain informed Hadley with a stern face of the cost of the motorboat in which he'd been heading out to sea. Then he broke into a big grin. "Hadley," he said, "I commend you. I couldn't have operated that thing. I don't know how in the world you figured it out." From that moment on, whenever the "motorboat crew" was called, everyone chorused, "Hadley, you're it!"

Noah's Ark

After his escapade, Hadley welcomed a period of relative tranquility, at which time the *Lanark* began to resemble Noah's Ark.

The ship had a mascot, a Spaniel named Perth, after

the Ontario town that donated it. "When we went down to Bermuda, it was as calm as could be and the dog got seasick," says Hadley. "But after that she never got seasick again, sort of got her sea legs." If guns were fired, Perth scooted like mad to the wireless cabin, where she stayed until the firing stopped. "I think the noise probably bothered her ears," says Hadley. Quite the canine sailor, she was able to climb straight up a ladder. No one ever complained about Perth or said she was in the way. Like Hadley, she was a source of comfort to many a sailor.

The second pet came on board as the ship left Londonderry on Boxing Day 1944. Boats came out to exchange turkeys or geese with the sailors for packs of cigarettes. "One of the fellows got a goose and asked permission of the captain to keep it as a pet," says Hadley. The captain said, "Permission granted, with one condition!" "Yes sir?" the sailor asked. "You clean up after it." The crew sailed with their menagerie for only a little longer before Europe and the war came too close for comfort.

Torpedo Hell

In January 1945, at the southern approaches to the Irish Sea, torpedoes hit two ships that the *Lanark* was escorting. The sailors were stunned. One of the ships was an American Liberty ship, the cargo workhorse of the United States Merchant Marine. It limped into port, fortunately without fatalities. The other was a Norwegian tanker that lost four men. The *Lanark* tried to escort it to Swansea in Wales, but it had to be beached before they could get it that far. The navy considered it a total wreck.

The event unsettled everyone, with faith or without. A few months later, on Hadley's second-to-last eastbound convoy, the resemblance to Hell came even closer. Twenty days before the war ended on May 8, 1945, his convoy was nearing the Bay of Biscay. "It was a gorgeous day," Hadley remembers, as he went on watch at noon. At 1315, while checking the most recent messages, he heard somebody yell, "Torpedo!"

Hadley thought, "This is it." But before his thought was complete, the ship's crew had snapped into action. The officer of the watch immediately thrust the *Lanark* off course. Every man on board ran to his appointed battle station. Prayers, audible and inaudible, were launched by believers and nonbelievers alike.

Hadley's action station, the quarterdeck, was in the aft of the ship. He had to run the full length of the ship to wait for further instructions that never came. From his station, Hadley could watch the tracks of the torpedo. With the *Lanark* off course, the torpedo traces were now heading for an American Liberty ship carrying cement and sugar. "It went down in two minutes," says Hadley. "I timed it from the time we heard the blast until it disappeared." As they watched in guilt, Hadley's crew knew the torpedo was meant for them.

Six men were killed. Fortunately, the others had a rescue

ship on the way. As the *Lanark* and the rest of the convoy sailed off, Hadley offered a silent prayer for the desperate plight of the fellow seamen they were leaving behind.

His prayers were rudely interrupted. An ear-splitting explosion accompanied the torpedoes that hit another ship in the convoy, a British tanker named *Empire Gold*. The *Lanark* was the closest escort to the ship, and Hadley saw everything clearly. The *Empire Gold* immediately broke in two. The tanker's cargo, identified as "10,000 tons of white spirit," as well as its own fuel, spewed into the ocean. "The flames just went sky high," recalls Hadley.

With ignited oil and gas floating on top of the water, the inferno was volatile. "We approached as close as we could, but the heat could've affected our ammunition, so there was a limit to what we could do," says Hadley. "There was no possibility of picking up people in that environment. It was absolutely unbelievably hot."

The tranquility and security of previous ocean crossings were replaced by horror, knowing it must have been Hell for the men of the stricken ships. "*That* shook our crew," says Hadley. "We watched men jump into the water and realized they were probably on fire. I was praying for these fellows." "I'm sure some of them burned to death relatively slowly. The fact that this could happen to me ... it was the first time I'd come across death in a gruesome way." It was the first time many of the men on his ship had witnessed what a torpedo could do.

Finally, after about 20 minutes, a lone sailor was brought aboard Hadley's ship. He was burned, but not as badly as three other men who were scooped up by the rescue ship. The remaining 43 boys or men — sons, brothers, and fathers — died.

Shaken and saddened, Hadley held on tightly to his faith. Its spiritual comfort was not for him alone. Sailors sought him out, wanting to talk. The *Lanark*, with its 160 men, was normally a hub of noise. "But we were a pretty quiet ship until we got to port in Londonderry, and the guys hit the bars," he says.

Goose down

After hardship, a sign of hope is supposed to appear. Instead, Hadley and the crew of the *Lanark* found themselves facing mountainous waves and gale-force winds in their next convoy crossing that February. The *Lanark* sailed with 85 ships, including 5 escort ships. "At the height of that storm we didn't see another ship, not one, for three days," says Hadley.

The captain gave orders that nobody was to be above deck except the officer of the watch and a duty signalman. The captain acted as the officer of the watch simply because everybody else was so tired. Hadley was duty signalman. "We got word that one of our convoy ships had lost all its boats and was taking water, and the captain decided that we were the ones to try and do something about it," says Hadley.

They were heading into the sea at a bit of an angle so that the ship didn't bear the full weight of the swollen waves. "In calm waters, we were 40 feet above the waterline," says Hadley. "But now, I could look out on either side of me and see water above us. I was hanging on for dear life!"

The compass arrow strained at the 45 degree mark and wanted to go farther. As soon as the captain gave orders to make a turn, he realized that they probably wouldn't make it. "He just looked at me and said, 'Hadley, I think we've had it,'" says Hadley. "We countermanded it immediately, started to turn a bit, then she slooooowly came back." At the end of his watch, Hadley went down to the mess deck. It was a shambles. "The men wanted to know what on earth we were doing up there," says Hadley.

They didn't hear anything from the other ships for days. Then they finally got a signal from the Azores, a group of volcanic islands in the northern Atlantic Ocean. "All the ships were scattered. It took us three days to gather everyone together," he says.

Their own ship had suffered significant damage in its unsuccessful mission. Even worse, their goose was missing! "We had fixed up a crate so it was sheltered from the wind but that whole contraption disappeared," he says. "We wanted to come into St. John's harbour with our flag at half-mast, but the senior officer wouldn't allow it," remembers Hadley.

Soon after that voyage, when the seas had calmed and the war had ended, Hadley returned to civilian life. He married Edna and with the help of his DVA credits, became a Baptist minister. He firmly believes that his two years at sea enabled him to be a better, more effective, minister.

Chapter 5
The Canadian Navy's Loss

Earl Wagner
[Master Mariner in the
Merchant Navy]

I n World War II, there were two navies, one more recognized than the other. The Royal Canadian Navy was the official *naval* branch of the country's armed forces, providing armed protection during the war and other post-war benefits to its sailors. Canada's merchant navy was really a navy of peaceful pursuits. But during wartime, it became the fourth arm of the service, as it transported equipment, supplies, and troops to support the war effort.

Merchant ships were far from adequately equipped, however, to protect themselves when U-boats and enemy surface vessels attacked. The Canadian Navy therefore helped to protect them in a system of convoys. Both navies served important roles during the war, so men with naval ambitions could choose to sail with either the Royal Canadian Navy or the Merchant Navy and see plenty of action.

The Royal Canadian Navy has its chance
From an early age, Earl Wagner dreamed of joining Canada's merchant navy — like his uncle. In West LaHave, Nova Scotia, he watched in awe as Uncle Earl came home on leave. The respect and fuss the master mariner garnered from family members on his infrequent short visits to shore made Wagner want to follow in his footsteps.

In Grade 6, young Wagner wrote an essay that described how he yearned to be a ship's captain when he grew up. But after graduation, he forgot his dream. He worked briefly on a farm, then in a lumberyard. By the time of his 16th birthday, however, he found himself once again looking longingly at the sea. People all around him were joining the armed forces, and he'd seen many family friends join the navy. He concluded that the quickest way to get to sea was to join the Canadian navy.

"The Royal Canadian Navy operated naval vessels designed as warships for high-speed manoeuvrability, fitted with weapons capable of fighting the enemy on the surface, under the surface, or in the air," says Wagner. During wartime, the navy's power was naturally compelling to a young man, so Earl applied for a boy seaman's position with the Royal Canadian Navy. When told that the navy "didn't require" boy seamen at that time, Wagner felt humiliated. He was told to apply again when he was 17.

With his uncle's example and stories in his head, Wagner was insulted they wouldn't give him a chance to work hard and prove his capabilities. He suffered in silence for a year. "Like most boys my age, in wartime, I wanted a job, or to join the armed forces," he says. After celebrating his 17th birthday, Wagner promptly applied to become a merchant mariner, turning his back on the Canadian navy. His only thought: "The Canadian Navy had its chance."

One hand for yourself and one for the job

Warmly welcomed by the Merchant Navy, Wagner discovered that this was the maritime force for him. This navy also boasted many types of ships. "There were tankers, troopships, freighters, colliers, and small coastal vessels," says Wagner. His first ship was the *M.V. Reginolite*, an Imperial Oil tanker that carried crude oil from the Caribbean to Canadian and American east-coast ports. It was fitted with a four-inch deck gun to defend against attacks from enemy submarines. In addition, the tanker had an assortment of anti-aircraft guns.

Wagner joined the *Reginolite* as an ordinary seaman, the lowest level of mariner. As he prepared to board the ship for the first time, his stomach churned with mixed feelings:

excitement, fear, and sadness. Guided by his mother, who saw him off, Wagner had packed enough clothing to survive the frigid Atlantic climate. "Heavy underwear, pants, jackets, a hat, oilskins ... and enough paper and supplies to write home," he says. But arriving on ship, he discovered some essential clothing was missing. He hadn't come prepared for the wetness! More experienced sailors told him what he needed, so Wagner disembarked. He quickly purchased a pair of sea boots, a sou'wester, and a rubber suit before running back to the ship. All of these items would come in handy in his challenging new job.

For the $45 Wagner was paid monthly, he was expected to do manual labour, keep the ship clean and well painted, and undertake dangerous jobs. "Seamen were expected to go aloft," he says, explaining they had to paint the mast, funnel, or the hull. "Most of the time you were swung from a bosun's chair, a wooden seat about 24 inches long and 8–10 inches wide."

The work started at the top of the mast or funnel, and progressed downward. "There's a good seaman's saying: You had one hand for yourself and one for the job," says Wagner. "One slip and you could fall 60 to 100 feet to the deck or into the ocean. If the knot slipped or you moved out of the chair, you didn't usually do it again."

To paint the sides of the ship, Wagner was slung over the side on a four-metre-long plank and lowered towards the water. A life ring in the water was tied to the deck. "That was about the only precaution they took," says Wagner. "If you fell into the water, you swam towards the life ring." Work like this developed his intestinal fortitude. Wagner didn't know it at the time, but he was preparing for the survival tasks — and other menaces — of convoy crossings.

Wagner became used to the dangers of the lines and ropes of the ship, too. "You had a 10-inch circumference line, that's about $3\,^1/_3$ inches in diameter," he says. "You get these things soggy and wet and they get pretty heavy. Then in the wintertime, they freeze, and they're not easy to handle." Wagner also had to hoist things up with big wires and handle cargo winches to swing cargo into or out of the hold of the ship. It wasn't easy work. A sailor could easily lose a leg or foot if he got one caught in a winch.

When not doing dangerous work, Wagner made friends with other boys on the ship. Because of the little space on board, recreational activities were limited to card games or a friendly boxing match. They often created friendly competitions to see who could paint or clean the quickest.

Hoping to make a career of seamanship, many boys were studying navigation. Along with reading books that taught signals, Morse code, or mapping, they learned by working alongside experienced sailors. Wagner learned quickly, and he was soon promoted to the next rank, able-bodied seaman.

"All seamen," says Wagner, "who had more skills and experience than ordinary seamen, sometimes steered the ship, but everyone took turns on lookout, in all kinds of weather." In wartime, merchant sailors had new navigational dangers to report — enemy aircraft, floating mines or torpedoes.

Wagner was a member of the four-inch gun crew that was supposed to defend his ship from submarines or surface raider attacks. "Surface raiders were battleships, or peace-time ships that kept their dummy superstructures so that they still looked like commercial or passenger ships, but were fitted with larger guns of 10 to 12 inches to outdo our 4-inch guns," he says.

Because of the war, Wagner was only 20 years old when he achieved a new level of expertise. He received his mates (home trade) certificate — a government certification that qualified him to serve as a third, second, or first mate on any type of ship in specified geographic waters.

Avoiding the bottom of the sea

Wagner then sailed as a ship's officer in the North Atlantic throughout the rest of the war. "I sailed in convoys that consisted of any number of ships from only a few to over 100 vessels. Ships, 400- to 500-feet long, massed together travelling half to one nautical mile apart ... that's about 3,000 feet, and spread out up to 100 square miles," he says. As prime targets for enemy torpedoes, bombs, and mines, they all had to be blacked out at night.

Though navigation in convoys proved to be an added difficulty, weather conditions in the North Atlantic — in

The four-inch gun crew

the form of storms, gales, fog, ice, freezing rain, and snow — always contributed to the challenge. "Vessel collisions between the convoy ships were common," says Wagner. Sailing close to one another, vessels rolled, pitched, and tossed about during bad weather. A malfunction of the steering equipment or human error made collisions likely.

But during the war, the merchant seamen's greatest fear was enemy submarines. If the enemy attacked and destroyed a vessel, the crew would be cast into lifeboats or life rafts where, if they were lucky, they were picked up by a rescue ship. Many were not lucky and perished.

"As young teenagers in war, we felt we were too young to die," remembers Wagner. "We thought that it would be someone else who would lose their life. But there was always that continuing, lingering, gnawing feeling ..."

In 1942, Wagner was shocked to see 14 Allied vessels all lying on the ocean floor along the Atlantic seacoast. They were partly exposed — and all in sight of land. Lying on their sides, or with a large air pocket keeping the front end partially afloat, he could see them clearly. "From the deck to the bottom of the ocean was about 50 feet, plus the mast, you could be looking down only 20 fathoms [120 feet].

"I will never forget the tragedy of lost ships and seamen by submarine warfare," he continues. "When you see 14 ships and their cargoes, and all the human lives that were lost, it's devastating. You see that many in a day and you start calculating the value of the cargo and ships you're talking millions of dollars worth of loss, plus lives that are irreplaceable.

"When you're young you think ... the other fellow got it, so I missed it. I'm lucky. Other times you have an anxious, distressed feeling ... you know that if your ship gets hit right below where you're standing ..."

The recurring fear was justified. Fifty-eight Canadian-registry merchant ships were destroyed in the war, and 1,146 Canadian merchant sailors perished.

Wagner lost many friends and relatives to the war. Some were buried in Europe; others were buried at sea, and the locations of their graves are unknown. Fortunately, his Uncle

Earl survived the war and, like Wagner, continued in the merchant navy. "As a merchant mariner in World War II, I felt very proud to serve my country," says Wagner.

The Merchant Navy's acceptance of him as an underaged sailor allowed Wagner to make a career at sea. "I served as captain on a 570-foot tanker of 18,000 tons, commanded several ships in the western Arctic, and I served as a ship's pilot, port warden, navigation instructor and managed a fleet of government ships."

The forgotten veterans of the unknown navy

After World War II, Wagner continued to fight a maritime battle — for merchant navy memorials, as well as recognition of the merchant navy's contribution to the war effort. "We really were the forgotten veterans of the unknown navy," he says. After nearly 50 years, Canada finally declared him and his colleagues Merchant Navy *Veterans*. Wagner was much decorated for his efforts and described as "the most knowledgeable mariner in the Maritimes." And to think ... he could've been in the Canadian Navy.

Chapter 6
Smoking Guns and Fires

Martin (Bud) Walsh
[Merchant Navy]

C onditions on merchant ships were arduous and dangerous for sailors early in the war. Until merchant sailors were able to depend on protection from the navy, they felt like sitting ducks for the enemy's submarines. But like their brothers in the Royal Canadian Navy, merchant seamen were proud of their important work and their tough vessels, and they were willing to endure the dangers for a life at sea.

Before there were enough Canadian ships to provide the Allies with desperately required goods, Canadian merchant sailors could find themselves working on foreign ships.

The Canadian government operated the merchant seamen's manning pools, which found crews for Allied ships. The pools provided sailors with room and board and a small salary to keep them around until a ship needed someone with their skills. Once their names were posted in a pool, seamen were allowed two refusals, then had to accept whatever ship they were assigned.

Manning pool

It was in 1942 that 17-year-old Martin Walsh first meandered through the Montreal manning pool, willing to take any work he could get. He heard that a Polish merchant ship docked in New York needed someone. Figuring he'd get Canadian wages, as well as the protection of the Canadian articles (a series of documented, beneficial working conditions), he signed on.

He discovered sailors of 10 other nationalities, each with their own mandated working conditions. The Polish seamen had the Polish union. The British nationals worked for British wages. Some crew members had been U.S. Immigration detainees given the alternative of going to sea.

After spending a year with the Polish merchant marines, shovelling coal into the ship's boilers, Walsh returned to Montreal, where he again signed on with the manning pool. While waiting for his next job posting, he received $13 a week, part of which he used to enjoy events in the army and navy club. Unlike other canteens catering to service personnel, merchant seamen were welcomed here. The main attraction was the price for a quart of beer — 40 cents.

Walsh and other merchant seamen also visited the nearby Molson Breweries. On the first two visits, they joined the brewery tour, which always ended at the bar. "When we showed up a third time for the tour, the attendant recognized us and sent us across the alley to the workers lounge with instructions to the bartender to give us two beers," says Walsh. From then on, he and his friends dropped in every couple of days to pick up their beer ration. The teenager thought life in the merchant navy wasn't so bad!

To discourage men from going elsewhere for work, pool sailors were allowed to undertake day labour for extra money while they waited for ships to arrive and post their requirements. Walsh worked in meatpacking plants loading frozen beef into railway cars and unloading slabs of bacon from brine vats where they had been soaked and cured.

"Any of these jobs would turn the average person into a vegetarian," he says. "Unloading vats of brine after the meat had been in them for two weeks would turn you off meat," he says. "I couldn't stand the look of the stuff. The fat of the meat had turned green, and I'd have to scrape it off to get the meat ready for market." What was the attraction of the job? He was paid $5 cash for a 10-hour shift, a small fortune to add to his weekly pool salary.

Training to shoot

To improve his employability with ships, rather than meatpackers, Walsh signed up for a gunnery course. Early in the war, merchant ships were unarmed, and the number of casualties was appallingly high. Sailors on ships carrying volatile cargo knew that if they were spotted by the enemy, their chances of survival were slim. As a result, despite limited cargo space, merchant ships began carrying guns and torpedo nets. Merchant sailors lacked combat and munitions training, so the Royal Canadian Navy began to supply several men for each ship to lead the maintenance and operation of the guns and train the merchant sailors as assistants.

In a specially built movie theatre adjacent to the manning pool, Walsh learned how to shoot down airplanes. After some instruction, the course participants were taken on a field trip to Mount Bruno. "We went skeet shooting with a shotgun on a pole to simulate a machine gun mount on the ship," says Walsh. Part of his training involved the identification of airplanes — their sounds and silhouettes — because the last thing anyone wanted was to shoot down an Allied airplane! For taking the course, Walsh was paid $10. His new skills would prove invaluable to any ship during the war.

Merchant ships were armed with a 4-inch gun aft, a 12-pound surface gun in the bow, and Oerlikon .20 calibre anti-aircraft machine guns. Walsh was now qualified to provide ammunition to the gunner. "It was a lot nicer to be able to work with the gun crews," he says. "When you were in those conditions, you wanted to do all you could to help. It was easier on the nerves if you were able to do something when under fire."

On April 12, Walsh was sent to Sorel, Quebec, to join one the many new coal-burning ships built for war, the SS *Whiteshell Park*. He went on board for its first cruise on the St. Lawrence River. Everything was clean, new, and smelled of fresh paint. For the first time, Walsh was on a ship with adequate shower facilities. He had a bunk bed with sheets and blankets, in a cabin with only four men, each with a locker and dresser drawer. "It remains, till this day, as my favourite coal-burning Park ship," Walsh says.

Under attack from within

Waiting for her cargo, the *Whiteshell Park* was ostensibly safe at dock in Montreal. However, Walsh already knew from experience that merchant seamen could sometimes face as much danger on their own ship as from any enemy.

The ship's fuel was stored on the upper deck in huge bins called coalbunkers. The fine coal slid down a chute from the coalbunkers into the boiler room, 12 metres below, where it was used as needed by firemen like Walsh. The stocks in the *Whiteshell Park*'s coalbunkers were low one day and in the cold weather, a crust had formed on the bunkered coal. It looked like a secure surface to walk on.

A first-time sailor, unaware of where he was walking,

crossed the crusted coal in the bunkers. Without warning, the sailor plummeted through the thin crust. "We didn't know anything was wrong till his feet came through the opening into the stokehold," says Walsh, who was in the boiler room below.

Until the men realized that they were not being attacked and didn't have to flee for their lives, chaos reigned. "There was coal flying all over the place," says Walsh, "as every man turned to with a shovel to dig this fellow out."

The man was eventually pulled free but not before the weight of the fuel had pushed the breath out of his lungs and rendered him unconscious. His nose and mouth were full of coal dust. One of the men cleared his airway passages and he began to breathe again. Much later, after he returned from the hospital, he told the captain, "I feel all right but I lost all my money when I was buried in the coal." Remembers Walsh, "The captain was so relieved to see him alive that he gave him $20 out of his own pocket." Within the hour, the sailor went ashore and disappeared for two days, returning just in time for the ship's departure. Walsh hoped he had both recovered and learned from the hard lesson — for everyone's sake.

The ship stopped briefly in Quebec City to install protection from the *real* enemy. Torpedo nets — large nets made of cable that could be lowered over the side in dangerous waters — were added to detonate and offset the impact from torpedoes.

Below deck on convoy

Three days later, the *Whiteshell Park* arrived in Sydney, Nova Scotia and, by May 2, had joined a convoy in mid-ocean on its way to England. Walsh was now ready for the strategic battle of the Atlantic, playing his important role from below deck. His dark and steamy boiler room was the width of the ship, with about three metres between the top of the boilers and the bulkhead. Its floor was below the waterline. Lighting was dim and everything was coated in black soot.

The most significant piece of safety equipment that Walsh had was a sweat rag tied loosely around his neck that he pulled over his mouth to keep the dust out. Even on this new ship, he didn't have safety glasses and didn't wear gloves. If he had to handle a hot bar or shovel, he flipped a cloth around it. He pulled ashes from the furnace, sweating bullets.

As the experienced fireman, Walsh coordinated the work on the three boilers. "To control the steam pressure, it was essential that the three men worked together," he says. Maintaining steam pressure affected the variable speeds required to maintain the ship's position in the convoy. If the ship got out of position, even slightly, it risked a collision. If the steam pressure got too high, it blew a safety valve. "The noise could be heard for miles on a clear, dark night," he says. It could alert enemy ships or submarines otherwise oblivious to the convoy's existence.

Smoke was also a threat to safety, not just to the firemen, but to the convoy in general. A plume of black smoke could draw the attention of distant enemy vessels. Minimizing smoke was both an art and a science. "The secret was not to pile too much coal on the fire," says Walsh. "Keep it light and hot and shovel less, but more frequently." As a result, the firemen got little rest during the dangerous convoy crossings.

The ship was controlled by increasing or lowering the revolutions of the engine, accomplished only with good teamwork and good communication between the bridge and the engine room. "It was a tricky task to maintain speed and position in rough weather with a light ship," says Walsh. His ship was often light. "We always returned from Britain with only enough ballast to keep the screw [propeller] under water."

"There was always the threat of danger," he says. "The escort ships were dropping depth charges almost nightly, indicating there was some reason to worry. The noise from the exploding depth charges was frightening to those working below the waterline, and if the explosion was close, it sometimes felt like the ship was getting hit."

False alarms

To lighten the mood during those worrying days aboard ship, merchant and navy ships always had pranksters among their crews. The same sailor who had fallen through the coal crust worked as a trimmer, shovelling coal in the bunkers. He had a fear of the ship being torpedoed so usually worked in the stokehold with his life jacket on. "Whenever it got too hot, he'd take his life jacket off, and then one of us would hit the side of the ship with a slice bar! It sounded like a depth charge," laughs Walsh. "The trimmer would scoot upstairs as fast as he could without his life jacket." Walsh knew it was a cruel joke, but necessary, if rare, entertainment for young men at sea.

The *Whiteshell Park* arrived in Belfast Harbour, Northern Ireland, late in May 1944. Walsh's ship normally went to Loch Ewe, but the sailors heard that Loch Ewe was crowded with ships awaiting a secret invasion. As it turned out, Belfast Harbour was also overloaded with ships waiting to convoy back to North America.

Two days later, in the middle of the night, Walsh's vessel was leaving the busy harbour when an American Liberty ship accidentally rammed into its right rear quarter, which was beside the crew's quarters. Walsh was asleep at the time in a bunk about 10 metres from the point of collision. He woke up and asked what had happened. "We've been in a collision," he was told. "Are we taking water?" Walsh asked. "No" was the reply, so Walsh rolled over and went back to sleep. When he got up in the morning and saw the damage, he was surprised he'd slept through it. He also realized how lucky he was to be alive. "The flukes of the anchor of the other ship had torn the handrails off the deck right over my head. The damage left a large hole almost to the waterline," he says.

On June 6, as the ship was being repaired, ironworkers hand-riveting new plates over the damaged area told Walsh about the imminent Normandy invasion. Ships had left the night before for the D-day invasion. What had been top secret was now the talk spilling from everyone's lips. Walsh's ship was returning to Canada, so while the information was interesting, his hope was that the invasion would make the seas safer to sail in again.

Finally, the ship could leave Belfast. Walsh had his 19th birthday at sea before arriving back in Montreal on June 16. He liked the crew and the ship so much that he signed right back on to the *Whiteshell Park* for its next voyage — another convoy bound for Britain. Arriving at Liverpool, the ship anchored in the River Mersey, waiting its turn to go up the Manchester Canal to unload its cargo.

Smoking off the job

Here, Walsh found relief from the fires in the depth of the ship. Since this was his second time in Manchester, he was seen as the expert to lead shore leave. "I knew all the spots where seamen could drink and be accepted," he says. "We could take a streetcar from Salford to Manchester and see a film with a live musical revue between the pictures. In the movie theatres, smoking was allowed. We thought this was great. We all smoked." It was typical of the time, and though Walsh spent his days as a fireman shielding his lungs from smoke, he thought nothing of lighting up a cigarette when he was off duty.

On his next convoy, Walsh was assigned to shovel coal on

the *Dentonia Park*, which had been launched August 7. The ship had made only one trip. What Walsh didn't know was that the ship's four-inch gun had not yet been properly tested.

As was the custom, the escort ship dropped a smoke float off to the port side of the convoy. As each ship passed the float, the gunners fired their guns at it. "Our big gun was mounted on top of the afterdeck house, a little square house at the back of the ship that contained the showers and washrooms for the crew," says Walsh. The seamen and firemen's mess was located immediately below the gun mounting. When the *Dentonia Park*'s gun fired at the float, asbestos insulation from the bulkheads and ceiling flew everywhere on the mess deck. Men screamed to get the target practice stopped. To Walsh's amusement, he had once again found himself under attack by his own crew. .

After four convoy trips to Britain during 1944, Walsh stayed with his ship one more year. His next two ships took him to warmer climates, where, with the war over, he was able to enjoy life as a regular merchant seaman.

Chapter 7
Cooking up a Good Time

Ken Farquharson
[Royal Canadian Navy V89650]

en handled the stresses of war in different ways. Some crumbled; others performed their assigned roles with meticulous precision, and many simply put on a brave face. Ken Farquharson was different. His positive approach, sense of humour, and adventurous spirit served as his personal strategies for coping with war.

With the approach of his 18th birthday, and compulsory service in the armed forces inevitable, Farquharson knew he didn't want to go to war. But in June 1944, he received his army call-up papers. Wisely, he solicited advice. He walked down to the Toronto docks, where he spoke to a recruitment officer on the HMCS *York*. "I don't want to be in the army," he said. "What should I do with these?" he asked, pulling out his papers. Without hesitation, the sailor told him, "Rip them up, and be here first thing in the morning."

So, Farquharson became a sailor. Some might say he went boldly into the navy but he saw it differently. "I was 18. I was young, and I was stupid," he says. "I had no fear of war because if my number was up, I could do nothing about it, but I had no room for fear. I had a duty to perform." Others might say he denied the reality of what lay ahead, but Farquharson's acceptance of his fate ensured memories of jovial, life-affirming experiences, with only the occasional interruption of breathtaking drama or sorrow.

Nine to five, with a few perks
With most of his time spent aboard the frigate HMCS *Sea Cliff*, Farquharson served 232 days at sea as a galley cook. The meal for which he was responsible was rotated. There were three other cooks on the ship, perhaps to ensure that the crew never had more than one bad meal in a row and that no cook ever got lynched. Compared to the duties of other sailors, the galley offered cheerful working conditions. Farquharson enjoyed being the ship's cook. "We had office hours," he says. When the meal was served and the cleanup done, he was on his own time until his next turn for meal preparation.

Farquharson still had to adapt to the tough life at sea.

Conditions were cramped aboard the *Sea Cliff*. Hammocks were strung two, sometimes three, high. "They were slung every night and stowed each morning to give more living space," says Farquharson. An early riser, Farquharson avoided the crowds for the morning showers in the ship's head (toilet), which could accommodate only six to eight men at a time. The sailors washed their clothes by hand or sometimes trailed them behind the ship. When the vessel reached its destination port, the sailors always had to help clean and gut the ship.

One day, the mariners on Farquharson's ship got some unexpected tender loving care. As supplies were being restocked and ammunition loaded in port, the men were all directed to leave the ship. To their surprise, they were taken to a deserted beach, where they were encouraged to lie back and enjoy the warmth of the sun — with all the beer they could drink. In the meantime, British members of the Women's Royal Naval Service (the Wrens) cleaned their ship from top to bottom. Farquharson could hardly believe his fortune: life was good in the Royal Canadian Navy.

Action stations

But navy life wasn't all sunbathing and beer. Farquharson's ship was assigned to escort and protect three convoys. The convoys comprised 20 to 50 ships that were spread over a large area. At times, the escorts weren't in visual contact with the ships they were escorting. If it made contact with the enemy, Farquharson's vessel was expected to leave the convoy and pursue the contact.

In addition to his regular work, every sailor had an action-station duty. When action stations were called, even the cooks quickly shut everything down in the galley and ran to their stations. In the event of fire or torpedo attack, sections of the ship were locked off to prevent the spread of fire or limit the intake of water. "If you didn't get out, you could be trapped in an area that was locked off," says Farquharson. Being trapped was a serious threat to life.

Farquharson's other job was gun layer. As the elevator brought the ammunition up to gun level, he took the shells off the elevator and handed them to another gun layer, who put them in the breach. The 4-inch shells weighed at least 23 kilograms, and depending on the number of rounds fired, Farquharson might perform up to 20 exchanges. He did the work with gusto — believing it was good work for his physique.

On monotonous days, the sailors used icebergs as target practice, firing the ship's guns to break them up. The icebergs were a hazard to merchant ships, and the activity eased the unnerving quietness of the transatlantic voyage — in addition to keeping the men's target skills primed.

They had to be ready for anything, including rescuing the enemy. Once, the *Sea Cliff* was escorting a convoy with the HMCS *St. Thomas*, a castle-class corvette. The *St. Thomas* made contact with a submarine. "She brought the sub up with depth charges ... When the submarine came to the surface, its men abandoned ship, and the *St. Thomas* sunk the submarine," says Farquharson. The *St. Thomas* then called on Farquharson's ship to help pick up the enemy survivors. None could survive in the cold ocean water for long. Some of the men were in lifeboats or wearing life preservers, but others just bobbed around in the ocean. "These men would grab hold of the scramble nets tossed over the side. About 20 were able to board the *Sea Cliff*," says Farquharson. "I thought, 'There but for the grace of God go I.'"

On board, the German sailors were put under military guard, and the *Sea Cliff* continued to sail with the convoy until it reached Gourock, Scotland. There, the prisoners were transferred to the care of the Royal Marines. Farquharson's ship continued on to its naval base in Londonderry, and better times.

Strike up the band and fire all guns

Around 0600 hours one day, Farquharson's ship was leaving the Irish Sea and beginning its journey up the Foil River. Further upriver was a naval Wrens base.

Some of the sailors on board who played musical instruments had formed a little "orchestra." As the ship slowly drifted towards the barracks, the captain mustered the four-piece orchestra onto the quarterdeck and ordered them to "Strike up. *I'm in the mood.* I mean it. I'm really in the mood!"

"Our old man was a playboy, and he'd spliced the main brace [shared the ship's rum] as we were going upriver," laughs Farquharson. In anticipation of shore leave, the entire crew had already got into the grog.

The ship's *woop-woop-woop* noise periodically drowned out the orchestra, but announced the ship's arrival to everyone for miles around. The Wrens were getting up for the day. "So the Wrens were hanging out of their barracks' windows, and they were waving their panties and their brassieres at us," laughs Farquharson. As soon as the ship docked, sailors rushed to find bicycles in hopes of returning downstream and finding the Wrens. The thrill of the chase kept everyone busy — and wore them out before they could realize the pursuit was hopeless.

While the sailors were stationed in Londonderry, they got bicycles again. Farquharson cycled as far as he could. "Londonderry was on the side of England, the rest of Ireland was not," he says. "We were told: do not wear your cap; do not cross over the designated area, or else you could be interned."

A short time later, Farquharson's ship was again sailing up the Foil River, and the captain had again spliced the main brace, before ordering the usual firing practice. Perhaps it was the influence of the grog, but without checking the depth of the water, the captain yelled, "Fire all guns!" The hedgehog, a forward-firing gun on the bow of the ship, fired about two dozen projectiles that went up ahead and then curved in a downward arc. If the projectiles didn't hit anything, they would sink to the bottom of the water and explode there.

The captain realized — too late — that his vessel was in shallow water. He rang down to the engine room, "Up revs! Up revs! Up revs!" This meant "Go like hell! Get out of here!'" recalls Farquharson. The hedgehog made contact with the bottom. "Our stern came right out of the water and back down again," says Farquharson. The captain was heard to utter, "Enough of that splicing the main brace!"

Get out of the way

It wasn't long before an incident reminded them they were at war. Farquharson's ship picked up a contact on a submarine. Depth charged, it was forced to surface. The submarine, however, had a bigger gun with a longer range than the four-inch one on Farquharson's ship. If the crew of the sub were instructed to man their deck gun, his ship would be outgunned. As the submarine surfaced, Farquharson could only hope that it would surrender quietly. But it was not to be. In the tense standoff, Farquharson's ship wired the nearby British striking force of destroyers for help.

"A destroyer showed up in no time," says Farquharson. It was travelling 30 knots (55 kilometres per hour) and was equipped with concrete in the front for ramming. "She hailed to us to get out of the way," he says, but Farquharson and the crew watched the destroyer approaching, not comprehending the instruction. The destroyer repeated, "GET OUT OF THE

WAY!" Suddenly the crew realized the destroyer wasn't slowing down. The crew of Farquharson's ship stood paralyzed as they watched the destroyer bearing down on the submarine *and them*, still hailing *"GET OUT OF THE WAY!"* A normal convoy travels 8 to 10 knots (15 to 19 kilometres per hour). Farquharson's captain had to struggle to put space between his vessel and the submarine. The destroyer rammed the sub. "She cut it in half," says Farquharson.

Grog and other comforts
Farquharson's ship continued to escort convoys between St. John's, Newfoundland, and Londonderry. Each time their ship docked, the crew found some way to celebrate their safe arrival. Sometimes when they arrived in St. John's, so many other ships were docked that they had to anchor out at midstream. Bumboats carrying Newfie screech came out to meet the ships and traded the grog for eggs. After a bottle of the liquor broke on the deck, sailors devised a test to determine its potency. Men made their guesses as to the percentage of alcohol in the screech. "A chap took a match to it," says Farquharson. "The liquor went up in a blue flame. It was almost pure alcohol."

In Londonderry, nearing the end of the war, American ships also tied up alongside Farquharson's. Although Farquharson thought he had a pretty good life on his ship, he was amazed to find that the Americans were better equipped. They had clothes-washing machines, potato peelers, and milkshake machines. They even had air conditioning and slept on bunks, not hammocks. "Jeez, we're fighting a war and you're on a cruise," he complained.

Eventually, without all the comforts of American ships, Farquharson took ill. He had slept outside on the upper deck and developed pneumonia. Drafted ashore, he was confined to a hospital in Sydney. As he recuperated, the young bachelor became friendly with a nurse.

After lights out one night, the nurse showed up with another young nurse and some "medicinal" rum for Farquharson and his buddy. "Let's go bowling," one of the nurses suggested, and Farquharson readily agreed. They were gleefully bowling grapefruit down the hospital corridor towards pop bottles when the officer of the day opened the door at the end of the corridor. "Farquharson," he bellowed, "I think you're well enough to return to your ship." The next morning, the fun-loving Farquharson was back on duty, escorting another convoy.

Surrendering sailors

Farquharson was in his beloved galley when news flashed through the vessel that victory had been declared. The joyous news was followed by a warning that the enemy might not observe it and to still be prepared for anything.

Eventually, out in the middle of the ocean, five submarines surrendered to his escort group. "They were hours apart, but I could see the submarines popping up. I suddenly realized: All of these were out there," he says. Some of the submarines had a device to outfox ships, a snorkel-like contraption that allowed them to cruise below the surface. If the sea was reasonably calm, the snorkel allowed them to stay below the surface and get air, yet not be detected. "We called them snorkel pigboats," Farquharson says.

From the galley on the upper deck, he witnessed the exciting surrenders. The boarding parties rowed across in whalers to gather important documents, secret information, and code books. They left a few Canadian sailors on board while putting the submarines on tow.

Once Farquharson's ship docked in Londonderry, the crew obtained bicycles once more and went back to tour the submarines. They talked with the enemy crews of the submarines. "And you know what?" he asks rhetorically. "They were just kids. Just like us."

With that sobering discovery, Farquharson's seafaring joys and dramas ended. Maintaining his sunny disposition, he accepted the offer of veteran's schooling and became a carpenter on land.

Chapter 8
The Gentleman Sailor

Tony Winstanley
[British and Canadian Merchant Navies]

o survive the hardships of life at sea, World War II seamen usually had to be rough-and-ready types. A resourceful lot — quick witted, and shrewd — they were often born tough. Tony Winstanley wasn't a typical seaman.

Raised in the Midlands of England, the son of a well-to-do farmer, Winstanley attended an exclusive private school. His refined manner of speech exuded "upper class" and reflected a man unaccustomed to rough weather, rough hands, or rough characters. As an English gentleman, Winstanley documented his unique observations from his seafaring career in a diary.

His youth was spent at a small Catholic boarding school for boys that was situated in the middle of 121 hectares. Parents and visitors arrived by car, and a gate porter ensured that only the entitled gained access to the grounds. Despite small classes and plenty of individual attention from the Dominican Fathers who ran the school, Winstanley unfortunately failed to make the academic progress that could justify the expense of the school.

His strongest memory of the school was the traditional and embarrassing "going-away chat," which was supposed to warn students of the undesirable company and temptations of the flesh that lay beyond the safety of the school property. With that auspicious farewell, 16-year-old Winstanley had to find work in the real world.

Stay away from the sea
On December 29, 1936, Winstanley's father escorted him to his first job — and his very first ship — the *Burma*. After a few private words with the chief officer, his father descended the gangway. At the same moment, an elderly seaman approached the younger Winstanley. "It was evident from his manner that he wished to help me," he recalls.

The old mariner told him, "Take my advice, son, before it's too late. Go back down the gangway ... Stay away from the sea!" He must have sensed the naive boy's unsuitability for the hard life at sea.

As the old man warned, maritime life was indeed a

form of shock treatment for Winstanley. "I didn't know port from starboard," he says. He served his first four years with no-nonsense sailors from the Scottish Highlands. They didn't hesitate to tell him he was "bloody useless."

When the *Burma* hit rough seas, Winstanley's head began to spin, his stomach churned, and his legs wobbled like rubber underneath him. The mariners accused him of trying to avoid work by feigning illness. Despite the humiliation of heaving his stomach contents in pitiful groans while the other mariners whistled and went about their daily chores, Winstanley tried steadfastly to grasp the essence of seamanship.

One of his early jobs was to relay orders shouted from the bridge — a peculiar job to assign a newcomer who was unfamiliar with nautical terminology. It may have been more than coincidence that his more callous colleagues chose to have him relay an order to "heave."

The verbal order to begin one of the many coordinated pulling activities on board ship — "avast heaving" — had become shortened to "vast heaving." Late one cold night, after an afternoon of vomiting into the ocean, Winstanley heard this order. Bravely he parroted, in his upper-crust English accent, what he thought he heard: "Ff-fa-ast heaving!" Fortunately it was too dark to see the rolling eyes of the other seamen, but Winstanley still heard their groans.

Throughout his seafaring career, Winstanley would continue to be dogged by seasickness, a condition that makes the afflicted wish it were fatal, if only to end the debilitating nausea and dizziness. With time and experience, however, Winstanley began to figure out some of the nautical, and human, nuances of the seafaring life that had been chosen for him.

Learning the ropes

In 1945, leaving Britain in a wartime convoy bound for Montreal, Winstanley boarded his next ship, the *Egyptian Prince*. By then he knew it was customary to report to the ship's captain. This captain, however, had a reputation for being conspicuous by his absence, seldom venturing out of his room. When Winstanley knocked on his door, he heard nothing for a moment, then the clinking sound of bottles. The door opened, and he was confronted by an attractive, but disheveled, woman. Winstanley, in his naiveté, assumed her to be the captain's wife. "She told me that her husband was resting, took my discharge book, and closed the door," he says. At the time he was still too unsophisticated to recognize her snickering sarcasm, but had Winstanley thought back to the going-away chat he'd received at school, he might have made the connection between this woman and the women about whom he was warned.

Through the school of hard knocks, Winstanley gradually learned the ropes and became determined to build an honourable career on the sea. He found assistance and friendship from other ambitious young sailors, such as Cadet

The *Egyptian Prince*

David Ffollkes, who was preparing for his second-mate's examinations. After putting in the required time at sea, the cadets went ashore to complete their studies and take gruelling exams. Winstanley took examinations many times to get entry into officer training and to improve his rank. "You went before a master mariner and gave answers to a drilling of questions on meteorology, rigging, how to make knots, signals, Morse lamp or Morse code, how to handle a lifeboat, what to do in bad weather, and many, many things," says Winstanley. "It was an awful ordeal."

Ffollkes wanted watch-keeping experience, so Winstanley joined him on the 8 to 12 watch. While Winstanley had never even had the benefit of a training ship, Ffollkes had attended a nautical school before going to sea. Winstanley soon realized that the cadet knew more than he did. "But to his credit, he never took advantage of this, and so we ran an efficient watch and both of us profited," he says.

Bridge watches in bad weather were uncomfortable, with or without good company. The wheelhouse was only partly enclosed; the after part was entirely open to the elements, but Winstanley knew to wear heavy clothing and oilskins. From serving on the *Burma*, Winstanley had learned the importance of not just being a good seaman but dressing like one, too.

Although the senior officers should have helped the inexperienced Winstanley learn this kind of practical information, they simply didn't have, or make, the time to do so. For a year, though, he had shared a cabin with a 17-year-old cadet. "He was very kind and decent," says Winstanley.

Because of the cadet's help, the gentleman sailor was better able to protect himself from other seamen's jeers. "The wearing of wristwatches or gloves invited derision," he says. "Even in the coldest weather, men wouldn't cover their hands as it was considered unseamanlike, and the only way one could get the feel of a rope and do a job properly was with bare hands."

From the cadet, Winstanley had learned other important things. Knives were carried in pockets, not demonstratively on belts. French berets were popular because they were less likely to blow away in the wind than other headgear. "A sou'wester was essential in heavy rain," says Winstanley.

"Sea boots were also necessary, but I was warned to be extra careful when wearing them whilst climbing down a ladder into a hold, as many men had fallen to their death that way," he says. "If a man fell overboard with sea boots on, he had to get rid of them quickly as it was almost impossible to swim with them." Fortunately, Winstanley didn't have to experience this firsthand.

Convoy to Canada

By the second day of sailing towards Canada, the convoy was organized, with all ships in position. The commodore of the convoy then ordered the ships to carry out a practice shoot. Gunners, like all marksmen, had to retain their skills to be ready for battle on the high seas. Nobody knew when the enemy would appear, so they took the opportunity to fine-tune equipment and synchronize actions when they could.

The gunners, seconded from the Royal Navy, manned a four-inch gun while Winstanley, as the junior mate of the merchant ship, served as gunnery officer. When the gun layer, the trainer from the Royal Navy, nodded to Winstanley, all he had to do was shout "Open Fire!" whereupon shots were aimed *between* the columns of the convoy.

The signal to fire went up from the commodore ship. The gun layer nodded to Winstanley. By this time, he had mastered relaying instructions, and to everyone's relief, including his own, he yelled on cue "Open Fire!" He plugged his gentleman's ears with cotton wool as the piercing sound of gunfire exploded around him. There were no disgruntled moans this time — Winstanley was getting his sea legs.

Because of his experiences, Winstanley could empathize with other under-prepared sailors, such as those in the U.S. merchant marine ship that had joined their convoy. Each ship's position was carefully monitored and reported daily to the commodore's ship. The bridges were always hives of activity at noon as the appropriate flags were hoisted to indicate their ships' estimated positions. An American Liberty ship positioned close to the *Egyptian Prince* was the only one never busy. "The commodore would have to then hoist a signal requesting the American's position, and after a significant delay, their signal would go up, giving a position very close to our own," says Winstanley. "Inevitably, we began to suspect that the American ship did not bother to work out a position but merely waited until signals appeared and copied them!"

Winstanley says it was rumoured that the U.S. merchant marine was desperately short of men during the war and that officers were being sent to sea as junior mates after only three months of training in an academy. "They were known as '90-day wonders,'" he says.

Despite his early trials, Winstanley was becoming an experienced and knowledgeable sailor. He continued to have difficulty with theoretical aspects on exams, but he was becoming adept at practical seamanship.

Winstanley's first transatlantic crossing convoy reached the St. Lawrence River intact, having fortunately avoided detection or enemy attack. His first time in Canadian waters he recalled, "Canada looked cold and bleak with a snow-covered landscape."

An atypical seaman

But Winstanley found Montreal to be "jolly pleasant." His British friends had given him a wish list when they heard he was sailing to Canada: silk stockings, jam, food luxuries unobtainable in Britain. "It was just good to walk around illuminated streets with no blackouts, and of course, the fact that there were no air raids was marvellous."

Dancing with girls at a Montreal seaman's club was another new and heady experience for Winstanley, because of his sheltered boarding school life. But while Winstanley was comfortable offering genteel chivalry to his dancing partners and sipping the night away on one drink, his fellow seamen often masked their insecurities on land by getting drunk. Winstanley, by contrast, was back aboard ship before midnight. He didn't consider it decent to be out prowling around in the middle of the night — an unusual seaman indeed!

The next day, a general cargo was loaded on to the *Egyptian Prince*, which then sailed to Halifax to wait for another convoy home. While the ship was lying in Bedford Basin, Winstanley heard the news that President Roosevelt had died: "Roosevelt was Britain's biggest friend and did more for Britain than anybody else. I was sad that he'd died."

Winstanley's ship was on another convoy in the mid-Atlantic when, again, the ship's radio officer received important news. This time it was good news — the war had come to an end. "The ships in the convoy blew their whistles, and the escorts fired off rockets in celebration. For the first time in four years, we turned on our navigation lights," he says. No longer worried about lurking enemy submarines, they could see and be seen. After five years of war, Winstanley and his comrades would not be bombed anymore, the forces would be going home, and the conditions of war had been lifted. Life would indeed be different at sea.

Business as usual?
That was all the celebration there was for the Royal Merchant Navy. When the convoy arrived at London, it was business as usual. "Merchant ships arrived completely unannounced; there was no ceremony. Good heavens, no," says Winstanley. "That's the difference between the Merchant Navy and the Royal Navy." Only representatives from the shipping lines were at the dock to meet Winstanley's ship.

When warships came back, people lined the docks and everyone waved and cheered. Merchant mariners in England, like in Canada, in spite of the important role they played in the continuation of commercial shipping, were an unappreciated lot.

Despite the end of war, Winstanley remained with the Royal Merchant Navy, still hoping by perseverance that he would accomplish enough to make his parents proud. Due in part to his favourable impression of Montreal, he emigrated to Canada in 1948. Winstanley continued to work diligently to become an officer and, in 1962, obtained his master's certificate — the ultimate ticket that acknowledged his abilities and entitled him to be captain of any ship afloat: a gentleman captain.

Chapter 9
Upwardly Bound

Ted Rushbrook
[Royal Canadian Navy V27245
Officer 0-64290]

W orld War II jump-started careers in the navy for many young men. Career advancement during the war was much quicker than in peacetime, so many young men in their late teens and early 20s held highly responsible positions. Coping with the responsibility during the intensity of war was never easy, but one youth who managed was Ted Rushbrook.

In 1939, Rushbrook had just completed his Grade 12 education. He spent the summer working as a copy boy for the Canadian Press and was at work the night war broke out. "Of course, I was gung-ho to enlist," he says. But his boss encouraged Rushbrook not to be hasty and to complete Grade 13, which he did. He was promised a job when he came back, which he thought would be the next year.

Officer aspirations

When he enlisted, Rushbrook, like many boys, wanted to be an officer at sea. He believed that war could be quite different from an officer's point of view, and he set out to work and study hard to achieve his goal.

Rushbrook started his naval training in 1941 as a wireless operator. Although he had signed up for the navy, the schooling qualified him to work in this position in any of the armed forces. At the end of his course, the instructors telephoned the air force and said they had 25 trained radio operators, where would they like them? When the air force said they needed cooks, not radio operators, the instructors offered them to the navy. The navy replied, "Send them down!"

"So we were in the navy," says Rushbrook. Initially classified as a lowly ranked seaman, Rushbrook went to the University of Toronto for three more months to study the physics of sound and learn how to make radio transmitters and receivers. In the evenings, he went to Western Technical School for electrical wiring, tinsmithing, woodworking, and cabinet making.

Rushbrook was sent to Halifax to train as an asdic operator since that equipment could be used to transmit messages underwater in Morse code. Then for two months he enjoyed work on deck, while his vessel, the *Baddeck*, was in refit.

One evening, Rushbrook was surprised to be called to the wardroom. The first lieutenant told him, "You're going in front of a selection board tomorrow morning, young man. You'd better have a drink. You'll do better if you've got a hangover." But Rushbrook disagreed. He always pocketed an extra 10 cents a day from the navy because he didn't drink his tot of rum. He also wanted to be on his toes because the selection board chose prospects for officer training.

Passing the test, he was given the choice of going to King's College in Halifax or Royal Roads on Vancouver Island. In March 1942, he became a student in the last class of reserve officers to graduate from Royal Roads Military College.

Learning on the job

As a new officer, Rushbrook was posted to William Head, British Columbia, to serve as the stores officer. "I didn't know anything about store keeping," he says. In Rushbrook's inexperienced view, he had a petty officer to look after the supplies for him. But when it came time to move base, Rushbrook was expected to do an inventory. He discovered brooms, mops, and a multitude of odds and ends missing. He went to the captain of the base. "Here's my inventory and here's what's missing. What do I do now?" he asked.

The captain took pity on the new officer and advised Rushbrook that the items in stores were going to be transported by three landing craft over a two-day period. "You're going into an awful lot of rough weather. I think you might lose something overboard," he said. And just like that, Rushbrook's lost inventory was made to disappear.

"When we got up to Comox, I reported what we had left. I set up three stores and appointed a storekeeper for each one. I gave them a book and said, 'Now that's everything that's in there. It's yours. If somebody takes something out, you get a signature for it. If he brings it back, you sign it back. If you don't and it's missing, it's out of your pocket.' I never had any more trouble with stores," he says. Rushbrook was only 21, but he was catching on.

Next, Rushbrook was posted overseas for anti-aircraft training in Tobermory, Scotland. During target practice, a drogue, which is a funnel-shaped device towed by an airplane, was used. The seamen were instructed to always lead the target, which meant to aim ahead of the target so that they would hit the target when it reached the spot they were aiming at. "One day somebody was a little overzealous in leading the target. The pilot got out his Aldis lamp and signalled down 'I am *pulling* this blankety-blank target, not pushing it!' That's where the term 'friendly fire' originated from," Rushbrook laughs.

The big secret

In February 1944, Rushbrook was sent to Falmouth, a secret military base and repair depot situated at the entrance of the

English Channel. He knew he was being sent there to support some sort of amphibian invasion, but he didn't know when and where the invasion was going to take place. That wasn't revealed until the night before the event.

An older friend from Royal Roads, Charlie Bond, was to be the commanding officer of a landing craft and Rushbrook his second-in-command. They picked up the Royal Navy landing craft in terrible condition: it had already been used in North Africa, Sicily, and Italy. As executive officer, Rushbrook had to muster the crew each day and assign them jobs of maintenance and repair to get the craft ready for what they eventually found out was to be the Normandy invasion.

On June 4, 1944, troops were loaded into the landing craft, ready or not. The starboard ramp immediately jammed. Without thinking, Rushbrook grabbed a crowbar and, standing in line with the ramp, yanked the crowbar to free it up. It released and ran over Rushbrook's foot. The half-ton weight of the roller split the flesh on his foot. Rushbrook thought he'd lost his toe. "I couldn't feel anything except blood sloshing around in my rubber boots," he says.

At about the same time, one of the stoker mechanics was coming up out of the paint locker. The door unlatched unexpectedly and came down, and its clamp broke two of his fingers. "So after we got our troops on board, he and I were sent ashore to hospital," says Rushbrook. Ashore in Southampton, vehicles, troops, and activity were everywhere. When the men got to a hospital, a nurse asked them, "Is the invasion on?"

"We were sworn to secrecy," says Rushbrook. "We couldn't talk about what was going on, so we said, 'No, no, it's just another rehearsal.'" The two men were returned to their ship, Rushbrook's foot swathed in bandages, the other man's hand in a cast. There was no time for recuperation.

The 185 troops with full gear, plus folding bicycles, were waiting on board Rushbrook's craft for a full day. The invasion was originally scheduled for June 5, but due to bad weather, they had to wait a day near the Isle of Wight. Late in the afternoon of the 5th, Rushbrook saw ships of every shape and size imaginable — 4,000 of them — going across the English Channel from southern England to France.

"The vessels started on each side of England, east and west coast, went down to the English Channel, went along till they came to Southampton, and off Southampton, there was a huge buoy, a central buoy, and everything led to there," he says. Canadian mine sweepers had swept across the English Channel to France and put small marker buoys all the way across. Rushbrook's craft followed these to minimize the multitude of dangers they were already facing.

Rushbrook was resigned to the fact that he might not return alive. Before he'd set sail, he'd taken the precaution of packing all his gear and taking it to his wife's aunt, who lived in Southampton. He left everything with her in a sea chest.

On the morning of the invasion, Rushbrook, wearing

a huge headset with earphones, sat up on top of the bridge on the starboard side. He was connected to all the gun positions, the engine room, and the rest of the ship, to relay the captain's instructions.

Normandy Beach

Rushbrook's group of landing craft strayed dangerously close to the left-hand side of the swept area of the channel. A British destroyer returning to England was just outside the area and hit a mine. Rushbrook watched from his perch as the destroyer's bow dropped, and a big puff of smoke came out of the smoke stack. "Without a signal, our 12 landing craft altered course 45 degrees to starboard into the centre of the channel, straightened out, and kept on going — as though a signal had been given. It perked us up a bit. We were on our toes after that," he says.

As they were going into shore, Bond spotted a tetrahedral. "They were like oversized railway ties, and they were all done up in a cone shape with explosives attached to them," Rushbrook explains. The one that Bond spotted had already been hit by a small landing craft and demolished. Bond guessed that there would be no mines left on it. "So he just headed our landing craft for that tetrahedral, and we went in right over top of it," says Rushbrook. Even without mines, the tetrahedral put about six holes in the bottom of the landing craft! "We had a double bottom, but at least two of the railway ties came right through to the engine room."

Another landing craft came in on their port side and did hit a mine, blowing a hole in its forward troop compartment. Again, fortune prevailed. "Nobody was injured because standard procedure when we were going in on the beach was to clear the forward troop compartment and put the men on the afterdeck behind the metal plating," says Rushbrook.

When the mine exploded, however, Rushbrook's craft was sprayed with shrapnel. Bond, standing at the port side of the bridge, should have been protected by the chest-high, four-inch reinforced concrete, encased in quarter-inch armour. But the blast came over the top of the protective shield. Shrapnel entered Bond's neck, barely missing his jugular vein and stopping short of his spinal cord. Rushbrook, atop the bridge taking photographs, noticed Bond lying on the deck. "I was just about to say 'What the hell's he doing down there?' when I realized he'd been hit," he says. Two other seamen had also taken shrapnel.

As if Rushbrook didn't have enough to deal with, his craft had more problems on the beach. "We were bobbing around because the seas were running pretty heavy," he says. "One of the other landing craft collided with us." The vessel smashed into the port side, damaging the port ramp. "We were all in side-by-side on the beach. This clown came in from the port wing right across everybody's stern, out to the starboard end of the flotilla, and dropped his anchor there, locking us all in with his anchor cable." Because of the other ship's error, when the craft went in on the beach, only one ramp could be used. "It took longer to get our troops off," says Rushbrook.

Now, neither Rushbrook nor the fleet of landing craft could get off the beach because they were boxed in. Rushbrook wanted to cut the line so that everyone could get out. Instead, for reasons Rushbrook has never been able to fathom, the flotilla commander ordered Rushbrook's kedge anchor line be cut.

As his craft started to reverse, it sheared off its starboard propeller on the tetrahedral. The craft was left with only one propeller instead of two. "We didn't have the kedge anchor so that we could swing around, and the sea was pushing us in on the beach," says Rushbrook. "We ended up broadside across the stern of another landing craft and put more holes in our port side."

Eventually the craft was able to back away from the beach and — punctured like an old tire — return to England. It took two days in dry dock to get the craft seaworthy again. Rushbrook then picked up another load of troops and was back in the shuttle service.

Convoy training

In September 1944, after his last trip on the landing craft and a leave in Canada, Rushbrook was posted to a frigate for convoy duty. He boarded the river-class frigate HMCS *Teme*, which had been built for the Royal Navy but traded to the

Royal Canadian Navy. Rushbrook was acquainted with its recent misadventure.

"In July 1944, while I was still doing the runs across to Normandy with troops, the *Teme* had been in a group of ships, including an aircraft carrier, that was doing anti-submarine sweeps through the Bay of Biscay area," says Rushbrook.

The *Teme* got an asdic contact on a submarine and signalled so to the group. The standing rule was that all other ships were to stay out of the way. "Well, unfortunately, the aircraft carrier, which had an admiral on board, didn't," says Rushbrook. When *Teme* altered course to port to go after the submarine, the aircraft carrier rammed right into it. The bow of the aircraft carrier hit the ship behind the bridge on the port side, cutting through to the keel. Tragically, four men were lost.

By now, Rushbrook was a little more experienced. He and the *Teme* headed to HMS *Summer's Isle*, a Royal Navy training base in the Outer Hebrides, Scotland. Commodore Stevens, an admiral pulled out of retirement, was in command of the base. "He did a tremendous job of training," says Rushbrook. A typical manoeuvre started at 0800 hours. Stevens would say, "Okay, you've been torpedoed aft by an acoustic torpedo. Here's what you do."

The men had to rig up an emergency generator on the upper deck. They had to shift ballast forward into the bow in order to get the nose down and the back up as high as they could. Then they shifted all the ammunition. Everything they could get up to the forward part of the ship went up. At 1600 hours the commodore would say, "Okay, secure." And then they had to put everything back again because at 0800 hours the next day, they were going to have another exercise.

"One of the typical things he would do," relates Rushbrook, "... on a training run, he'd walk around on deck, see some seamen sitting around with nothing to do. He'd take off his hat with all the gold braid on it, and he'd throw it over the side and yell 'Man overboard! Don't just stand there! DO something!' Of course," says Rushbrook, "when he yelled 'Man overboard,' the ship would have to come around and we'd have to go through the entire rescue procedure. But he put us through this exercise of being torpedoed, and it was the best training you could imagine."

No false alarm

In 1944, Rushbrook appreciated the training when his ship, the *Teme*, really was torpedoed. He was on one of four frigates escorting a convoy from Londonderry south through the Irish Sea and around to Portsmouth. Rushbrook's ship was the trailing escort. Because of that position, he could not use the cat gear — a noisemaker that acts as a decoy to acoustic torpedoes. Extremely vulnerable without it, his ship had also been in asdic contact with a submarine since the early hours of the morning.

At 0720 hours, Rushbrook was on the edge of his upper bunk, getting ready to go on watch. He heard a *whoomp*, then a bunch more, but assumed it was a false alarm like they'd had on another realistic drill the previous month. "The navigating officer on the lower bunk was going out the door while I'm still sitting there," says Rushbrook. "Over his shoulder he shouts, 'That was a torpedo, son.'" Rushbrook slipped from his bunk into his boots, grabbed a life jacket, and followed him out the door.

It had been an acoustic torpedo. The sub with which *Teme* had made asdic contact earlier had taken refuge on the bottom of the Irish Sea, close to shore, with lots of rocks and wrecks around it. The *Teme* couldn't depth charge it in that location. Although the *Teme* had held the submarine down for an hour, the commodore in charge of the convoy finally said, "Okay, forget him. Leave him. Rejoin the convoy." As soon as the engines of Rushbrook's ship revved up, the submarine fired the acoustic torpedo. "It just homed in on the sound of our twin screws," says Rushbrook.

The torpedo exploded right underneath the quarter-deck and blew 18 metres of the stern away — and four members of the crew. "Three of them went into the water. We didn't find them," he says. "One of them was blown up on to the top deck behind the after gun. Of course he didn't survive."

However, thanks to the training by Commodore Stevens, everyone knew exactly how to respond. As the men ran to their "abandon ship" stations, the damage control group shored up the bulkhead between the inside of the ship and the Irish Sea. "If that had buckled, we'd have gone down like a stone," says Rushbrook.

As the men inspected the structure of the ship to determine how quickly she might sink, Rushbrook stood by his assigned lifeboat. He may have had officer's status, but he reacted like any young sailor, wondering what was going to happen next. "Once it was determined that we weren't going to sink immediately, the captain put us to work," he says. The men took measures to keep the ship afloat as long as possible, including shifting the ballast, as practised. Rushbrook was glad he had been trained for this. He was also happy to keep busy. "It kept my mind occupied," he says. Worries of the ship sinking — and his crew's fate — would have tormented Rushbrook.

Soon after this incident, Rushbrook was glad to celebrate VE Day in England with sailors of every rank. The only distinguishing characteristic they shared was that each man had lived to survive the war. "Officer or not, we all went through the same thing," he says. As a married man, Rushbrook was one of the wartime sailors who chose to leave the sea and seek a quieter life. He became a chartered accountant.

Acknowledgments

My sincere thanks to each of the men whose story appears in this book, but also to the others whose stories I couldn't include. In the course of research, I contacted dozens of maritime veterans who had great wartime stories, but alas, who had not been in convoys during WWII. As a result, I was unable to include them in this book, but perhaps in another ...

Some of the veterans with whom I made contact found it too disturbing to tell me their account. I wasn't able to connect with a few, for one reason or another. Several took pains to make sure I got their stories in their entirety and provided permission to use them. The stories, for the most part, came from face-to-face and phone interviews. A few men who had already written their own stories sent them to me, generously giving me carte blanche to do what I had to do in order to make their writings useable for this book. The written material ranged from one-and-a-half pages from one man to two books from another. The information for the chapter about Joe Marston was sent by his friend, Captain Hill Wilson, along with a heartfelt endorsement for its inclusion in place of his own story.

Special thanks to the following men for their generous permission to extract extensively from their writings:

• Tony Winstanley, self-published book, *Under Eight Flags*

Acknowledgments

- Martin Walsh, written recollections, "The North Atlantic in 1944"
- Earl Wagner, written recollections, "War-Time Merchant Navy"
- Hill Wilson, master mariner and editor of the *Red Duster*, the newsletter of the Canadian Merchant Navy Veterans Association, for the use of Joe Marston's recollections, "The Night of the Long Knives"

In addition, Ted Rushbrook rounded up friends Ken Farquharson and Jim McParlan and hosted an afternoon of storytelling in his living room! Thanks, Ted. That afternoon remains in my heart.

To each of the men whose stories are included, thank you. I am deeply grateful to you for being so generous with your time. I am also grateful for your patience and for your forgiveness as I stumbled over nautical terminology and showed my ignorance over and over again. In talking to each of you, and in working with your stories, you have become dear to me. I have tried to maintain your voice, for who can tell your stories better than you? If there is merit in these stories, it belongs to you. If there is error, or inaccuracy, the fault is mine.

My appreciation to Linda at The Memory Project, Mark at the Veteran's Alliance Web site; Janice Summerby at Veterans Affairs; Captain Hill Wilson; Lieutenant Commander Hubert Genest, Royal Canadian Navy; and Roy Finlay, president of the Canadian Merchant Navy Veterans Association.

Sincere thanks also to Sandra Phinney, whose support and friendship bring colour to my world; Joyce Glasner, for your insight and encouragement; editor Jill Foran, for your input into my previous book; editor Joan Dixon, for your patience and meticulous input into this one. Dan Streeter, you're a great man. One of few. Very few. The *Journal* is fortunate to have you. And of course, Lambros.

Further Reading

Collier, Dianne. *My Love, My Life: An Inside Look at the Lives of Those Who Love and Support our Military Men and Women.* www.mylovemylife.ca

Winstanley, Anthony F. (Tony). *Under Eight Flags, Vol. I, 1937–1947, The First Eleven Years at Sea.* Victoria: self-published, 2000. (available at: Under Eight Flags, #206, 1950 Bee St., Victoria, BC, Canada V8R 6P5)

Winstanley, Anthony F. (Tony). *Under Eight Flags, Vol. II, 1948–1957, The Next Ten Years at Sea.* Victoria: self-published, 1988. (available at: Under Eight Flags, # 206, 1950 Bee St., Victoria, BC, Canada V8R 6P5)

About the Author

Dorothy Pedersen is a freelance writer. She is the daughter of Archibald McInnes Thomson of the 52nd Anti-tank Regiment of the Royal Artillery. Her father's willingness to depict his war experiences without censorship gave Dorothy a glimmer of insight into the psychological impact of war. She found history books abandoned the human impact of war in favour of strategies, statistics, and military leaders.

Dorothy wanted to know more about the thoughts and feelings of people who were given a uniform and sent overseas. No one seemed to know, or those who did know didn't want to talk about such things or weren't encouraged to do so. But abiding by her father's teaching ("If you're not honest, you're nothing"), Dorothy tracked down real-live men — mariners — who had been in the war and were willing to tell their stories with honesty so that other people could learn what war was really like.

Dorothy is also the author of *Stolen Horses: Tales of Rustlings and Rescues*, in the Amazing Stories series.

Photo Credits

OTHER AMAZING STORIES®

These titles are available wherever you buy books. Visit our web site at **www.amazingstories.ca**

New **AMAZING STORIES®** titles are published every month.